DR. WILLI

A FIGHTER &
Champion

AUTOBIOGRAPHY *by*
DR. WILLIAM M. COMFORT
INCLUDES TESTIMONY BY DR. SHIRLEY COMFORT

DR. WILLIAM M. COMFORT

A FIGHTER &
Champion

AUTOBIOGRAPHY *by*
DR. WILLIAM M. COMFORT
INCLUDES TESTIMONY BY DR. SHIRLEY COMFORT

ANOINTED ROSE PRESS™

ANOINTED ROSE PRESS™

The Anointed Rose Press name and logo are registered
Trademarks of ANOINTED ROSE PRESS™

DR. WILLIAM M. COMFORT©
- A Fighter and Champion -

Dr. William M. Comfort
E-mail: ncbibcol5@aol.com
Office Phone: (410) 634-9005

ISBN-13: 978-0-9826841-5-3
ISBN-10: 0982684150
© 2011 by Dr. William M. Comfort

Anointed Rose Press
P.O. Box 21371
Philadelphia, PA 19141
E-mail: anointedrosepress.@gmail.com

Library of Congress Control Number: 2011902175
Library of Congress Catalog-in-Publication Data

Comfort, Dr. William

Dr. William M. Comfort, A Fighter and Champion / Dr. William M.
Comfort
ISBN (trade pbk.: alk. paper)

1. Autobiography   2. Spiritual

Cover Design: THE PRINTED WORD, INC.
Philadelphia, PA (215) 224-5500

 PREFACE

... Dr. William M. Comfort ...

I wish to make it very clear that I would not have wanted any other mother or father than the ones God gave me. They were perfect for my life. My father, William Henry Comfort, as you will see, was a man who was not afraid to face difficult situations. He passed that quality on to both of his sons. My mother, Beatrice Canazzaro Comfort, had an iron will. I saw her fall down some stairs when she was in her seventies and a dog chain ripped the flesh off her leg. She got up and shook it off like nothing ever happened. She had more shock treatments than I could ever count. After a shock treatment she would get up, shake her head like nothing ever happened. I was told by the nurses at Elmira Psychiatric Center, "Don't get in her way when she's determined to do something." She passed those qualities on to her children. If it were not for my stepmother, Roxie King Comfort, we would have never moved to North Carolina. It was there that I heard the Gospel of Christ preached. All three parents were God-sends in my life.

The Lord Jesus Christ saved me when I was seventeen years of age and totally at the end of myself. He put in my heart a passion to grow, learn, and build disciples. That was fifty-eight years ago. As a result of His working in my life I have been blessed with seven academic degrees and two fellowships. One of the fellowships is from Cambridge and the other is from the Oxford Educational Network. Only Jesus Christ could take a young man who was not a good student in school and fill him with these achievements. I also thank all the wonderful people along the trail that have encouraged and blessed my life. They are too many to even mention here. I am humbled and overawed by the love and grace of the perfect God-man, Jesus Christ. It is through Jesus Christ that we are more than conquerors because He lives inside the human heart.

Dr. William Comfort
President, Chesapeake Bible College
Ridgely, MD

A WORD FROM DR. SHIRLEY COMFORT

... Proud to Be His Wife ...

The first greatest thing that ever happened to me was when I received Jesus Christ as my Lord and Saviour, at the age of 13, at the Birchwood Baptist Church in Elmira Heights, New York. The second greatest thing that has ever happened to me was when I married Billy (Dr. Comfort) on February 5, 1960. I have been on the most glorious, exciting journey that anyone could take! I'm not saying that it all has been a bed of roses, as being in full time ministry together for over 50 years has been filled with many challenges! I will say this though: God has never failed us one time. Yes, we've had many tough times, but He has helped us get through them all. We have grown in our walk with the Lord together, as we both are totally committed to the Lord and to each other.

It was a total miracle how God brought us together, as we were many miles away from each other. I had met him in my home church in Elmira Heights, New York, when I was still in high school. He had been invited there by one of our young men, Terry Doane, as they both were going to college at Bob Jones University, in Greenville, South Carolina. The thing that I admired about Billy was his passion and love for God and also his passion to win souls to Christ. I graduated from high school in

1954, and went off to Canada to London Bible Institute and Theological Seminary. I was preparing to be a foreign missionary to French West Africa. After I graduated, my life took a different turn and I ended up in Fall River, Massachusetts teaching at one of the earliest established Christian Schools, in the fall of 1957. I had been there around a year when I got a letter out of the blue from Billy Comfort who was in Norfolk, Virginia working in a Christian Servicemen's Center. He and some other men had opened this center up trying to reach the Navy servicemen who were stationed in the Norfolk area. Well, I was totally surprised to hear from Billy after so many years. I had forgotten about him and had gone on with my life. I had dated several other young men by that time and had just broken up with Harold Corry, who was a businessman from Fall River. We were seriously thinking about marriage but somehow it became clear to me, that he wasn't God's choice for me. The principal of the Christian School where I was teaching was praying against this relationship, as she did not think that he was God's choice for me. So the relationship dissolved, just before Billy started writing to me. This was definitely God's timing!

We then began writing to each other for about a year. He came up to Fall River to see me a few times and we both realized we were meant for each other. I had received a full 4 year scholarship for Gordon College in Massachusetts and wanted to continue my education there. Billy said he would wait 4 years for me to complete my education, and then we could get married. So I completed a full semester, and on the Christmas break I got a ride to Norfolk, Virginia with some students who were from there, to visit Billy and see the ministry that he was in.

On Christmas Eve, he surprised me and gave me an engagement ring. He had already asked my father for permission to marry me on one of his trips to Elmira Heights, New York. I remember how happy I was when I went back to college and showed off my engagement ring to all the girls in the dorm. Somehow I didn't have as much interest in college as I wanted to be with Billy. I was almost 25 years old now, and I was ready to be married, and so was Billy. So we decided to have the wedding on February 5, 1960, the following year. We were married in my home church, Birchwood Baptist in Elmira, Heights, New York, and I started a whole new life with Rev. Billy Comfort.

What a journey this has been! I said I never wanted to be a pastor's wife but that is what I became for many years, as we pastored several churches in Virginia and Maryland. I loved being a pastor's wife and was very fulfilled in that role. The Holy Spirit has led us step by step, as I look back on our lives together. We raised our two sons, Derrick and Paul, in the ministry, and it was tremendous training for both our sons. They both are great men of God and are raising their children in the nurture and admonition of the Lord. Billy was a tremendous father to our sons and taught them the Word of God, not only from the pulpit but in everyday life. Both our sons are very successful in life and are filled with the wisdom of God. Our grandchildren, all 14 of them, are

God centered and are going to be greatly used by God in years to come. Billy and I are very proud of them!

Billy is my hero in every way and my best friend. He has always encouraged me in my personal life and in my education. I now have a PhD which I never dreamed I would ever have. I used to be very shy but he has brought me out of that shyness and helped me to have more confidence. He has always encouraged me to pursue the things that I am interested in, like the area of nutrition. I am in the process of getting my second Doctorate degree in nutrition. He has been my spiritual mentor in my walk with the Lord.

Through the years, we have become so close that we even think alike. My love for Billy grows every day. I gave Billy a Christmas card this year of 2010, and it said these words: "Thank you for being my husband, my partner, my friend... my "yes" when everything else is no... my calm when everything else is crazy... This Christmas, I just want to say thank you for being who you are... for being the kind of man who can laugh at himself... a man who works hard... who still finds time for his family. I just want to say Merry Christmas and I love you... today... tomorrow... forever."

Ephesians 5:25-31.... "Husbands, love your wives, just as Christ also loved the church and gave Himself for her, that He might sanctify and cleanse her with the washing of water by the Word, that He might present her to Himself a glorious church, not having spot or wrinkle or any such thing, but that she should be holy and without blemish. So husbands ought to love their own wives as their own bodies; he who loves his wife loves himself. For no one ever hated his own flesh, but nourishes and cherishes it, just as the Lord does the church. For we are members of His body, of His flesh and of His bones. For this reason a man shall leave his father and mother and be joined to his wife, and the two shall become one flesh." Billy has lived these verses, as he has always loved me unconditionally. We have truly become one flesh, as I cannot think of myself apart from him and he cannot think of himself apart from me.

He has always cherished me, and this is what every woman wants in a marriage. I am a very fulfilled woman because God brought Billy into my life. I love you Billy, and will love you forever!

Dr. E. Shirley Comfort
Vice-President, Chesapeake Bible College
Ridgely, MD

 FOREWORD

... Rev. Derrick M. Comfort ...

"A Life Lived for Christ is a Life Worth Living"

One of the distinct memories of my childhood was *my father* fearlessly sharing his faith. In my father's first church, Victory Baptist Church in Chesapeake, Virginia, he trained teams to go out every week and share Christ door to door. He built up a small church to one bulging at the seams with new converts. He preached Christ like Billy Sunday, pounding the pulpit and calling all who would hear to Christ.

After six years of exhausting labor, my father moved on to a large Southern Baptist congregation as an associate pastor. He took charge of the church outreach and started a bus ministry to bring people to church. There was a large community of lower middle class, as well as neighborhoods of "well to do." My dad took this on with a passion and was visiting as many as sixty people a week.

Soon the bus ministry went from zero to five buses filled with children and families coming to church. My father would leave early Sunday morning like a field commander going out into battle. He would even go into homes and help moms get their children dressed to get them on the bus.

Soon, both sanctuaries were full. Children filled the old sanctuary where my mother told stories of the Bible with flannel graphs that kept rapt attention. I remember those stories fondly, from Samson to Calvary.

All around me the Gospel was preached; from my father's many sermons, to my mother reading through the Story of the Bible, to listening to Billy Graham on that old green radio, while eating that delicious cheddar cheese I snatched before my mom used it in the mouse trap on our old country lane.

My father began sharing the Gospel immediately after he was miraculously drawn and converted to Christ at an open air street meeting while serving in the Air Force. In time, he and some other friends started the Christian Serviceman's Center in Norfolk, Virginia, right outside Norfolk Naval Station. They'd share the Gospel on the street corner with servicemen from all over the world, from big Turks to small Chinese, as the old song says.

They'd invite the men into the Serviceman's Center for games of ping pong, checkers and refreshments. They reached out, befriended them and shared the Gospel. My favorite picture of my father is the one you'll see sharing the Gospel with a sailor with an open Bible in his hand. No matter where we went, from the restaurant to the dry cleaners, my father was befriending people and giving them a Gospel tract.

I watched him share Christ with militant Muslims and arrogant Anglos. He was not ashamed of the Gospel of Jesus Christ, because he knew it was the power of God to save.

The day in which we live seems another era from those days so long ago, yet so near. Our nation and most churches seem to have forgotten the power of Christ to seek and save the lost. We are ashamed of the Gospel. We seek acceptance of the world and no longer are the Salt and Light.

Faithful men at Bob Jones University fanned his flames for the Gospel and passion for the lost. In the course of time, my father led his family to Christ. The faithful sharing of the Gospel from him and his brother, led my hardened grandfather to Christ.

My grandfather, Bill Comfort, was a light weight boxing champion in the Army. He trained with Rocky Graziano, and went on to fight ninety matches in Madison Square Garden. He went from hard living and being a Brooklyn brawler to spending his latter days as a faithful deacon, serving his neighbors and pastor in Elmira, New York.

One of my dad's early converts was his brother, who followed him to Bob Jones. Surviving on the mean streets of Brooklyn, Ron was soon singing live on radio and TV. Hailed in Nashville as the "Boy Wonder of the South," he left it all behind and gave his life to Christ. Like my father, he preached and sang Jesus Christ on every street corner and later around the world. Dr. Ron Comfort founded Ambassador Bible College in North Carolina that continues to send out powerful preachers and soul-winning evangelists for the Gospel.

This testimony you're about to read is more than a legacy. It is a challenge to our generation and those yet to come. If two little boys, from a broken home, lost, crying on the streets of Brooklyn, New York, can do this for Christ, what can you do? When I think of this, I am reminded of that scripture, "One will put a thousand to flight and two will put ten thousand to flight."

We never know what one man's faithfulness will bring. And because of One Man's faithfulness, even Christ, we have found grace and mercy even unto the saving of our souls from eternal death and damnation.

My father has a little saying, "Straight ahead every day." He still lives his life "straight ahead;" not looking behind. I can honestly say he was no hypocrite. I watched my father every day and he lived what he believes.

He has lived that old glorious hymn:

"I have decided to follow Jesus,
I have decided to follow Jesus,
I have decided to follow Jesus.
No turning back. No turning back."

Rev. Derrick Mark Comfort
November, 2010

 FOREWORD

... Dr. Paul W. Comfort ...

My father, Dr. William Michael Comfort, made an indelible mark on my life and shaped my early years significantly. He did this by living an example, by sharing his life and experiences with me and by offering me opportunities for leadership at an early age.

Our family life was based around church. Having my father as a pastor in a closed environment such as our church world made me the son of an important leader. So I was offered close access to leaders and gleaned from them. I was also offered opportunities for input on church problems. We shared them as a family often times after our family devotions and it helped shape my identity as a problem solver and helped me feel more grown up and comfortable with adults at an early age. Later in my teen years I took leadership roles in church programs and ministries. All these led to great development in leadership skills provided by a father who included me in his life.

My father's primary gifting is that of a teacher. He spent much time teaching us deep scriptural doctrines and truths. I have calculated that in my lifetime, I believe I have listened to close to 5,000 sermons...many of them his.

My father's profession was also his ministry. That helped shape my worldview that we should choose professions that allow us to integrate our lives. Our work, no matter what it is, can be a ministry. Our lives should not be divided into secular and sacred if we are to have a unified, focused life.

This book is the story of my father's life. He has always been very focused and driven in his ministry. He lived a life of integrity and truly practiced what he preached. I remember thinking that my father was perfect, because I never really saw him sin.

My father loved us, provided for us, and taught us as much through his example as through his words. I have always counted on him for guidance, wisdom and scriptural insights. I love him, honor him and respect him for all he has accomplished, for all he is, and for the imprint he has left on my life and therefore, my children's lives and their progeny.

The lessons you can learn from Dr. William M. Comfort's life are many including: always seek to continually improve yourself to make yourself more valuable, try to do one thing at a time and do it well and if you pour your life into others, it will come back a thousand fold.

Blessings,

Dr. Paul William Comfort

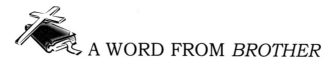 A WORD FROM *BROTHER*

... Dr. Ron Comfort ...

Four children were born to William and Beatrice Comfort. Eleanor was born in 1933 and less than two years later, William Michael entered the family. In 1938, Ronald George was the third in the family; and finally, in 1940, Constance Veronica was the final sibling of the four.

As Billy was four years older than I, I always looked to him as my example... (*See back of book for Dr. Ron's complete comments*)

Through the years our relationship has remained strong. God has led us into different avenues of ministry, but we have remained very close. Anyone who has been around Billy has been strongly affected by his soul winning zeal and his love for the Word of God.

In 1989, God led me to start Ambassador Baptist College. The college is simply for the purpose of training young people for full-time Christian service. From the first twenty years of the college ministry, more than seven hundred graduates and former students are involved in ministries around the world. Had it not been for the influence of my brother, Ambassador Baptist College would never have been established. How exciting it will be when we get to heaven and realize all the multitudes that have been influenced through the life, testimony and ministry of Dr. William Comfort...

Dr. Ron Comfort
President, Ambassador Baptist College
North Carolina

xix

 TESTIMONIES

...To me, Dr. Comfort is...

Although Billy and I have not been raised together, he has become closer to me than most people raised together. We have a very strong connection. We are both very comfortable talking to each other and loving each other as the sister and brother we truly are. He is a shining star. Billy is a wonderful example of life and loving the Lord and so is his most precious, wonderful wife, Shirley.

Connie Caggia
Sister

****

Dr. Comfort has been an inspiration and a joy to my life. At one of the most challenging experiences of my life he was there and helped me through. God bless Dr. Comfort and Chesapeake Bible College.

Apostle C. C. Carter
Presiding Prelate Apostolic Fellowship of Five-fold Ministries.
M.Div.MCC DD

****

Practically anyone who has accomplished much in life can point to a significant person or two that made all the difference—especially during the difficult phases and challenging stages. These mentors and coaches are rarely in the limelight themselves; their reward is the success and achievements of the ones they have poured themselves into.

Dr. William "Bill" Comfort is one of those mentoring, life and ministry coaches. It quickly becomes obvious to any observer of his lifestyle that this man literally lives to make others succeed. Nothing makes him more excited and energized than helping some person living below his or her potential get a fresh wind and achieve what had seemed highly unlikely or even impossible.

Many dreams that had died in the wastelands of routine and basic survival have risen from the dust under his guiding hand. His quick assessment ability enables him to identify and revive the innate, God-given abilities that have never theretofore been discovered or have lain dormant under the layers of one's misgivings. He speaks lovingly of those whose lives he has impacted as if they were his very children—or perhaps grandchildren.

It has been my privilege to know and work with this Man of God—this general of the Faith—for two decades. He and his precious wife, Shirley, have been great encouragers of Joan and me. Their indomitable spirits continue to energize us and humble us. We are in covenant together and I am sure we got the better part of that arrangement!

Bishop J.R. Pierce
The Love Church, Horseheads, New York
Love Aflame! Worldwide, Horseheads, New York
August 27, 2010

****

I am thoroughly delighted to have this opportunity to share my deep gratitude and appreciation for the life and work of Dr. William Comfort. From our first meeting until now, I have come to realize that it was not just a chance encounter, but a divine appointment. I am positive that this is not just a unique experience to me, but to many individuals in this country and around the world. I and many others are ever indebted to him because of the great sacrifices that he and his wife have made. Jesus said that the greatest form of personal achievement is that of a servant. Dr. Comfort continues to display that great gift to the world each day of his life. He is not just a servant, but one that our LORD says is profitable. He goes above and beyond the call of duty.

Dr. Comfort as a teacher, mentor and leader has helped us to achieve an accredited chartered school of our own. He has also made this possible for my friend Pastor N. David in India, and also Pastor Ondimu of Kenya. I have found that personal achievement is not just personal. I say this because when I walked down the aisle to receive my Masters Degree and Doctors Degree my family and some members of my church observed this. These moments were points of reference in the minds of all that experienced it. The sound of that experience resounded through various corridors of my family. Words could never express what a life like Dr. William Comfort has.

If I am allowed, I will use that famous term that has characterized all of Dr. Comfort's speeches over the years - "WOW." Thank you for this opportunity.

Dr. Richard A. Jones
B.A., M.A. Rel., Th.D.

****

In this day and time few men have the integrity, morals, ethics, wisdom, and leadership gifted to this one man.

Dr. Comfort is my mentor, my life coach, and spiritual Dad. Dr. Comfort is a soul winner, a modern day disciple for Christ, who builds leaders with a burning desire to share Christ throughout the entire world.

THIS makes Dr. Comfort world class, loved by many, and a true friend of mine.

Dr. John T. Jennings III
Dr. Chiropractic, B.A. Science,
Owner of AdjustFirst, LLC of Kent Island and Denton

****

For several years I have known Dr. William Comfort and he has been a fighter for the truth of God's Word and is a Champion in the true sense of the word. Not only is he a spiritual fighter but he is one who fights against physical conditions. He has the testimony as that of the apostle Paul—he will let nothing separate him from the love of Christ.

It is most encouraging to have a mentor who is a champion for Jesus and has a mind to never give up but is determined to fight the good fight of faith.

Dr. Samuel L. Dixon
Pastor/Overseer of M.F. Chase Unity Memorial Church, Star Hill, DE
Founder of the Interdenominational Bible Institute.

****

Dr. Comfort has been a friend, an encourager, and a true child of God. I appreciate this opportunity to share my true feelings about this man of God.

As you honor him in his life story, I trust that all who read it will be truly blessed as he has been a blessing to so many. He is so deserving of this book, and I pray it will top the sales chart.

May God's blessings be upon him, Dr. Shirley Comfort, and the entire Comfort family!

Dr. Gary W. Burns
AA; BA; MSL; DD

****

I came to know Dr. Bill in the 1980's. Seeking relationships with other Christian leaders, God brought him and Dr. Shirley into our lives. They have remained fast friends for nearly thirty years. Dr. Comfort and I, along with a significant group of other leaders, walked together through some very troubled waters. In the end, his friendship remained as others faded into the memories of times gone by.

Because of his encouragement, I pressed through to a doctor's degree. The programs he instituted became the foundation for the Georgia Coastal School of Ministry, just one of the many campuses that have become a part of his legacy. As a Christian leader, Bill has remained a compassionate and determined soldier of the cross; never flinching from difficult struggles, never yielding to a compromise of the Gospel.

As an educator, Dr. William Comfort has long sought to provide academic opportunity for every member of the body of Christ who desires to deepen their knowledge of God and His Word. Not only that, he has worked tirelessly in providing meaningful academic recognition. Through the work of Chesapeake Bible College and Seminary, Dr. Comfort has seen a vast fulfillment of his vision to recognize the academic work of hundreds of Christian leaders.

He should be able to lean back and appreciate God's great work in his life. Unfortunately, he is not. Instead, he is faced with the struggle of his life, a devastating bout with cancer that has racked his body with pain and strapped his finances to the breaking point. A lesser man would quit. But not William Michael Comfort. He has used this challenge to dig down deep and produce some of the most significant work of his entire life.

Always an optimist, filled with faith and perseverance, my friend, Bill Comfort is an inspiration, a mentor, a true soldier of Christ, and a brother in every way. I sincerely believe God will totally heal him, and his productivity will continue to the day he departs this life for his eternal reward.

Dr. Philip Byler
(Star Christian Network.org)

****

I have been amazingly blessed and favored by God to meet Drs. William and Shirley Comfort when I was spiritually like a thirsty soul in a desert. Having a God-given persistent inner drive for quality Biblical Education for myself and others, and having received little support in this area of ministry from local associates; I was brought directly to a fountain of crystal clear and clean "ministry of teaching" of the Word of God. The Comforts became to me like "rest" in a weary land, and a gusher of water in a time of drought. I am honored to be under their spiritual covering, and I consider them as my spiritual parents. I thank God for them each and every day. Dad and Mom Comfort, I love you. To God be the Glory!

Dr. Vicki Warner
(New Life Evang. Ministries)
Philadelphia, PA

 Chapter 1

My mother was a full blooded Italian, and my father William Henry Comfort was of English descent. The name "Comfort" comes from two Latin words; "con" which means with or together, and "forte" which means strong. The name means "together strong." I was born in Brooklyn, NY on Labor Day. I was a four pound premature baby born suddenly at home after a seven month pregnancy. My father said that I was so little that he could hold me in one hand.

As for my early life, we were basically victims, victims first of the "Great Depression" and then later World War II. Work was hard to get in those days, and from 1929 to the late 30's, men would do anything for work. In order to appreciate the background that I was raised in, you have to understand a little about Beatrice Canazzaro and Bill Comfort. Beatrice was born into an Italian family and her father Michael Canazzaro really didn't want her; he wanted a boy. He was very brutal to her when she was a child because he was so discouraged by the fact he didn't have a baby boy.

When parents didn't want their children, (specifically girls) in those days, they would take them to the Roman Catholic convent, which is where my mother was raised. The conditions behind the walls formed her mental pattern. Consequently, she felt very secure when she was in an environment that didn't have much interruption, but was a quiet sedate environment. She was a very intelligent lady; she spoke three languages at age 17. She could speak French because she was in a French convent; she could speak Italian, Sicilian if you please, and then also was very fluent in English.

My father was the black sheep of his family. His father Jesse Comfort married Lula. They didn't stay married too long; they divorced, but they had one son together. That was Bill Comfort. Lula remarried a fellow by the name of Russell Anders, and Russell Anders had children by Lula. But my father was the half breed in the family. Russell didn't care for him. My father, as a young boy at the age of 14, was doing man's work. He wasn't allowed to go to school very much. He was on the road picking huge boulders out of the road and helping construction people build highways in Pennsylvania and in New York.

My dad really didn't receive much love from his father and he didn't receive any love from his step-father. Even his mother wasn't particularly fond of him. He was always running away from home. (I'm telling you all of this so that you will understand how Bill's sons, Ron and Billy Comfort, were raised.) What happened in this situation was that during one of the many times that my dad ran away from home, he ran away with the circus and took a job as a handler of snakes. The circus travelled all over, and finally they went back to Elmira, NY.

My dad's mother came to the circus and just happened by the snake pit. There is her son Billy in the snake pit handling snakes, and she screamed and went into hysterics. She grabbed him and took him home. He was 14 at that time. Well ... things didn't go too well, but he endured it as best he could. When he was 17, he ran away from home again and got a barmaid to sign the permission for him to go into the army.

This is where things heat up a little bit in our background. My father was stationed in Camp Dix, NJ{now known as Fort Dix, NJ} One day as he was walking to chow, a big soldier in front of him stuck out his leg and tripped him. My dad fell face down on the concrete, but when he got up, the other guy hit the concrete. Bill cut him to ribbons, and then they went to chow.

After chow my father was summoned to report to the commanding officer. The officer said, "I saw what happened out there and I know that it was his entire fault." He also said, "You are a fighter", but my dad said, "No sir! I'm a lover." The officer said, "No, you're fighter and I want you to report to the gym."

From then on my father's duty at Camp Dix was to be a prize fighter. He trained with Rocky Marciano, who later became the middle weight champion of the world. Dad developed the same style as Rocky ... he was a body puncher and he would bob and weave. He had very short limbs and a long body so it was very difficult to ever tag him. At best, most men just hit the top of his skull.

He wound up in Madison Square Garden, with over 90 fights there winning records. In those days they would fight once a week and sometimes twice a week in Madison Square Garden. He started out with four rounds and worked his way up to either 8 or 10 rounders. I'm not sure which, but anyway, he was a fighter. As you may know, Madison Square Garden is across the Hudson Bay, so one day my father was going across the bridge on a bus. He was still in the service at the time, when Beatrice Canazzaro and Bill Comfort met on the bus. By then my mother's father had come and taken her from the convent, and she lived at home with him and his new wife. Eventually Bill and Beatrice got married and moved to Elmira, NY where my sister Eleanor was born. Times were very hard so they moved back to Brooklyn where I was born. At this point the story gets a little messy.

My father got a job as a bartender in a bar and he was making good money. The patrons were the Mafia. He got along alright, but one day he got word that the Mafia was going to kill him because he had overheard some of their plans. So, my father left the bar, went straight home to Mom and told her that he was leaving "right now" for Elmira, NY! He said, "Here's some money; take Eleanor and Sonny (me) and get on a bus and meet me in Elmira." He said, "I'm leaving right now."

Mom met my dad in Elmira and he did everything he knew how to do in order to make money. He sold fruit, was a door to door salesman, became a black faced comedian, and played in bands. He did all kinds of things to make money to put food on the table for his family. We were raised Roman Catholic and we went to a Roman Catholic school. My birth certificate said "William Comfort, Jr.", but when I was baptized Roman Catholic as a baby, I was given the middle name of my grandfather. I became William Michael Comfort.

Life was really hard in those days; and boys were always fighting. My dad got me a pair of boxing gloves for my birthday, and for Christmas he got me another pair of boxing gloves. He would put me on ... well, on one occasion he was showing me how to fight in our living room. He had a pair of training gloves and in the middle of them there was a piece of metal. My dad said, "Come on Billy, get tough," and he slapped me across the face with that piece of metal in the middle of the glove. Well... I got tough. That doesn't mean that I beat up everybody that I ever fought. I got beat up more times than I beat up the other fellows, but I remember that I fought almost daily for one reason or another. I don't mean that I wasn't afraid, but I did get tough.

Meanwhile, my father was "fire" and my mother was "gasoline", and there were always explosions in our home. Our home was very chaotic. My mother had problems with hydrochondria and she was always imagining things. On the other hand, my father had a quick temper and he would get mad at anything. Our home was unbearable. There was always arguing and fighting, and my dad was always going to bars on the weekend. My dad was a bar room brawler who loved to get drunk and fight. Beatrice, my mother, had an obsession to keep everything spotless. She would embarrass Dad by actually sweeping up cigarette ashes while the men were present.

They argued about Dad's weekend drinking spells and they argued about his spending money on beer. He and his cousins were called the "Dunkels". Dad and the "Dunkels" brothers would dress up in black and go to a beer joint. They would pick a fight with the drunks that were at the bar. The bartender would call the police and Dad and the Dunkels would spend the night in the jail. Then he would be in jail and we would go get him. This was a weekly occurrence. My mother's nerves could not adjust to this style of living so she began drinking.

 Chapter 2

Finally things got so bad between them that my father decided to go back into the army. Mother's nerves went from bad to worse when Eleanor was born. My dad had Mother committed to Binghampton State Mental Hospital in Binghampton, NY. When I was born she was all right. When Ronnie was born, she went insane again and was re-hospitalized. Connie, her youngest daughter, was beautiful and Mom loved her. We all loved my little sister because she was so wonderful. Connie was born in Elmira NY, on August 1, 1942, and was baptized Roman Catholic at St. Peter & Paul Church.

We had been living in a small town outside of Elmira called Horseheads, NY. We had a little house and there was a road that came through, and there were the railroad tracks. We moved often and every time we moved to a new house, I always got into a fight. The guys in the block had to see if they could beat me up. One of boys took a horsewhip and gave me a thorough beating.

My father went back into the service and my mother had just given birth to Connie and was overwhelmed with life. Ronnie was born, and was now around six years old. The next thing I knew, my mother decided that we were going to move back to Brooklyn NY. My mother had a yard sale and she essentially gave away everything; getting enough money for us to get back on the bus and travel 300 miles to Brooklyn.

We went to live on Atlantic Avenue. We had no furniture and no father. There were four children, with no income and no father. Mother got an apartment in a building that was infested with cockroaches; they were everywhere. We had no furniture, so we slept on the floor. We had no money coming in, so whatever we could scrounge to eat, we did it. We're now in a new neighborhood and it's my opportunity to be initiated into the new neighborhood. A group of boys came around me when I went outside to play and said, "we're gonna beat you up. If you cry, we're gonna beat you up more, but if you don't cry, we'll stop beating you up." So they beat me up real good, I sniffled real good and then I sucked it up and swallowed it all.

Eventually I got adapted to the area. One of the biggest events was to see boys in a fight. Everybody would always egg you on. I remember there was a boy that I really liked; his name was Joe Bodino. I really liked Joe and I wanted to go to a movie, but for some reason we got in a fight. I don't know why, because all I wanted to do was to go to a show. Joe was a little smaller than me and they all wanted him to win since I wasn't a full blooded Italian. So, I told him that I really didn't want to fight. I just wanted to go to the show.

Well anyway, I got in a lot of fights in that area, and I could tell you so many stories. I was walking down the street one day in another new neighborhood and this big boy by the name of "Crow" came up to me. He was a little younger than I but he was a big boy, and he had a real good reputation in the community on how he could beat up people. That day I was feeling real strong and I put a hurting on him. When he quit, the neighborhood boys called him "yellow" and "no good." Then they said to me, "Go on kid, you can walk through the neighborhood." So, that was one fight that I won.

What would happen is that you would get in a gang and you were always looking for mischief, always looking for something to do. One day the guys decided they would rob this fruit stand and of course, I was with them. Here is this nice man and he's trying to make a living selling fruit. We walked up and the next thing you know all of us boys have taken fruit and are running off with fruit in our pockets; and the man is screaming and hollering. We're about half a block down the road, and one boy said the cops are coming. So every boy drops his fruit on the ground. I look around and I'm the only boy left. I said, "I'm not giving up this fruit, I worked hard for it." So I picked it up and put it in my pocket. The cops didn't come.

We were always moving in those days because we couldn't pay our rent. Somehow we were able to get into another apartment, but we paid one or two month's rent, and then we had to move again. My grandfather was a barber and he was also into real estate. After a while, my mother got the opportunity to live in one of his homes and we lived around the corner from the barber shop. While in Brooklyn, NY, I saw my grandfather and grandmother nearly every weekend. They would have the whole family over to their home for a Sunday afternoon meal of Spaghetti and meatballs, Italian bread and beer. When we moved into the little house that my grandfather owned, we saw him two or three times a week.

My grandfather tried to poison our minds against my father. He would say, "Billy, your father, he is a no good. He drinks like a fish". We did spend time with our cousins while in Elmira, but in Brooklyn we did not have much of a relationship with cousins on my mother's side. I really was not attached to my grandparents because my young mind was concerned about survival in the asphalt jungle.

At this time the war was on and there were sirens and air raids, and it was so much going on. My father was in the war and my mother was working in a defense plant. She was hurled out into the rough and tumble environment of loud noises. For some reason we were accepted in this neighborhood. We got along well because people knew our grandfather. There was a group of nice boys, but others were really bad boys. We would roam the streets, and we would go everywhere while my mother was working. We would go and it didn't matter where it was. Mom got home at midnight and by the time she got home; we had roamed the streets until 11:30 and pretended that we were asleep. She would come home with fear in her eyes because she was afraid for her safety. Her nerves were on edge most of the time. Mom felt very good about her obedient boys, but we were really sneaks.

Mother had a lot of pressure on her and she would get mad. When she did, she would hit us with her fists in the face. One day I stood up to her when she tried to hit me and I told her if she hit me, I'd hit her back. It got out in the neighborhood that I had stood up to my mother, and these boys told me that if they ever heard that I was standing up to my mother, they would knock my lights out. The boys in the neighborhood carried knives and we were real poor, so I didn't have a knife. What I had was a fingernail file. In the place where we lived we had a tree, and for hours I would throw the fingernail file into the tree trying to get it to stick. I kept that file with me in case I needed it for self defense.

Even in my grandfather's house, my mother couldn't pay the rent. She had an allotment and was working but she didn't know how to handle money. She would go to the bars and blow the money, so we had to move again. This time we didn't have a whole lot; we could carry it on our back. We moved to Liberty Street which wasn't too far from where we had lived and there was a tailor shop downstairs.

Chapter 3

Then all of a sudden, my dad got a medical discharge and he got out of the service. He had a jeep turn over on his leg. I need to say this - during this time homes were being broken up. My father had been unfaithful to my mother and she was unfaithful to him. Mother had men and my father had women. My father became stationed at a hospital called Oteen in Buncombe County, North Carolina. The war was coming to an end and my father was getting out and he decided that he's coming back to his wife. When he returned it was the same as it was before, with arguments and fights.

Then my father decided to bring Roxie, his girlfriend, back and let her meet my mother. What happened? They meet each other and when she came to the little apartment, my mother got a butcher knife and came at her. But Roxie was a tough woman. My mother, at five feet, was no match for her. My mother was lying on the floor in a pool of blood, knocked out. Dad didn't know that she was pregnant with her fourth child when he enlisted in the army, and now she was left lying on the floor. That was the end of my parents living together. Dad and Roxie returned to Elmira, NY. Dad got a divorce from my mother and he married Roxie. Roxie worked as a presser in a dry cleaners plant and she could always get work. She worked at this occupation for over fifty years, and was very good at it. Roxie was a very strong person, and they lived on Pine Street.

 Chapter 4

Meanwhile, Mother couldn't pay the rent so we moved again, this time to Hendricks Street. It was the worst street that we ever lived on, for violence. In fact, prior to us living there, there was a man who sat in the back seat of a car with Tommie guns. He and others would spray bullets in the area, and there were a lot of gang wars. To say that the neighborhood was violent was using a mild word to describe it. Connie was two years old there and she was a very beautiful little girl. Then I was ten, almost eleven and Ronnie was seven and Eleanor was twelve and Connie was two. Little Connie is such a beautiful child. As for my mother at this stage, things are getting worse and worse for her. When Connie was born, Mother was all right mentally. Her mental condition grew worse when we moved from Elmira back to Brooklyn. While In Brooklyn my mother grew worse because she was the sole parent in the home and had great difficulty in raising the children.

She was alone and had no security; and when she would come home at night, she'd say, "Billy there's a man that's been following me." She was always imagining that people were following her, and she would go into rages. She was so fearful and emotional, and she would take a broom handle and beat my sister Eleanor over the back. My sister Eleanor died in her sixties, and until the day she died, she still had the welts on her back where Mother had beaten her. Eleanor was rejected by both my mother and father. She bore the brunt of being the firstborn and also of being a girl. She had very bad nerves all her life. Mother would punch us in the face if we spoke too loud or went from one room to the next. If we neglected to close the door, she would punch us out. If she had cleaned the floor and we got any dirt in it, she went into a rage and beat us badly.

I really tried to handle whatever came at me. When my mother would bring bums home, I would argue with them. It is a wonder that they did not injure me. When we moved to Hendricks Street, mother began leaving us alone in the house one or two days. The most that she left us alone was four days and there was no food in the house to eat during that time. We had a friend, her name was Mrs. Murray, and she tried to help us when she could. We had gone to the movies and had seen some horror pictures. When we were all alone in the house, I would imagine all sorts of murderers were coming to get us. One day things grew from bad to worse; I did not know where my mother was and I did not know what to do to help my brother and my sisters. So I went out into the busy street and sat down on the street corner and cried my heart out. I was expected to be the man of the house and I was just ten. I didn't know what to do. I didn't have any instruction on what to do.

The gang was very thick and close knit, and I was the new boy on the block again. So, when Ronnie and I would go out of the house, we had to fight. We could hardly walk on the street without somebody wanting to beat us up. Mother would say, "Go down the street and get me a loaf of bread." I would have to fight my way to get to the store. All you had to do was show up and somebody would say, "I don't like the way you look", and then you were in a fight. Things got really heated up in that neighborhood. There was a boy there by the name of Bobby, who was a great boxer and he was beating up Ronnie. I took up for Ronnie and then I got beaten up, so the boys in the neighborhood decided to initiate me. They tied my hands behind me and they tied me to a metal fence with sharp ends at the top. They decided if I passed, I would be accepted in the gang.

They tied my hands behind me and got a platter and filled it with dog manure. They said if I was willing to eat the manure, I would be accepted, and that would prove that I was a tough guy. In those days, I was very skinny and very agile. I could do all kinds of things with my body. I could fit into places where almost no one could get into. I could climb and so forth and I was very quick. I was able to break loose from the fence, but I pretended that my hands were still tied behind me. When they came with their offering, I kicked it in their face, jumped over the fence and ran into the house.

Afterwards, one day one of the boys saw me and began beating me up. Prior to this fight, my mother told us that she could no longer keep us and she was gonna send us to my father who was in Elmira, NY. I did not say anything to my mother because I did not want to get into an argument with her. My brother Ronnie and sister Eleanor were present when she announced that we would be leaving on the bus next Thursday. So, while this guy was beating me up, I stopped him in the middle of the fight. I told him that the reason he was beating me up was because I wasn't in shape; but if he would come back the following Thursday, I'd be ready for him. The guy said, "All right, I'll be back next Thursday and we'll see what you can do." I knew that I would be gone by then.

 Chapter 5

The following Thursday Eleanor, Ronnie and I were on a bus. My mother kept Connie because she was too little to travel without her mother. It was many years before we saw my sister again. That was one of the greatest hurts of my life. The greatest loss in the situation was not having Connie go with us. Connie was only two years old and my mother said that she was keeping Connie. Connie was adopted by my uncle Harry Canazzaro and was raised in a very lavish home. She was a beautiful girl but always felt the loss of her brothers and sisters. My mother was committed to Creedmoor State Hospital as a mental patient. Ronnie and I did not see Connie again until she was a teenager. Connie became a "grief counselor" in a large funeral home. We have not seen each other too much, but when we talk on the telephone, it is as though we never have been apart. My father never tried to get Connie back because she had a better home than he could give her.

Meanwhile, a new chain of events was happening. We got on the bus and traveled over three hundred miles to Elmira, NY. Along the way were bus stops so we would get off and go into the depot. We didn't have any money so I would look for toothpicks. I would put toothpicks in my pockets because I wanted to hand something to my dad when we met. Eleanor had long and stringy hair and the only clothes that she had was what she had on her back. I had a pair of shoes on, but one of the soles had broken loose from the shoes. I had a rope tied around my sole. All that Ronnie had was the clothes on his back.

Now Ronnie was always an extremely intelligent boy who had no problem making friends, and he was always somehow making money. I was never too good at that but Ronnie was. I guess I was good at keeping Ronnie from being beat up because I would take the beatings for him. I loved Ronnie...well, I loved my sister too; but Ronnie was the dearest thing to me. I loved him with every inch of my being and there wasn't anything that I wouldn't do for him.

When we got off this bus, there was nobody there - no Bill Comfort, no father. We kept walking around the bus station and there was nobody to meet us. Finally a policeman came up to us and said, "What are you kids doing here?" I told him where we had traveled from, and that our mother was sending us to live with our father. He said, "Who is your father?" I told him my dad's name. All of the policemen knew Bill Comfort because he had frequented their facilities quite often. He said, "Listen, we're gonna put you up tonight in a police shelter, and tomorrow we'll have your father come and you can live with him. I shall never forget this; the shelter was the cleanest place I've ever slept in my whole life. I will never forget how clean it smelled. They had a matron there and she was so nice to us, and they put us down in a clean bed. There were no cockroaches.

The next day here comes my dad and boy, did he look good to me. My dad was my hero, and my dad was so happy to see us. I didn't know what to say to my dad, so I said, "Dad, can I give you tooth picks?" Ronnie said, "Dad, do you have fifty cents?" Dad took us home to Roxie. She was from North Carolina and she really didn't want to live in Elmira, NY. So, she said, "Bill, this is no place to raise children; let's go back south. Let's move to Asheville, NC." If Roman Catholics were right, the most that Elmira would be was purgatory, but Brooklyn was hell.

 Chapter 6

Now my dad had a problem because he now has five mouths to feed. Now he calls me "Billy", no longer "Sonny". We got off the bus and Dad has nothing but 25 cents in his pockets, Roxie has an aunt, Myrtle Robinson. When I mention her name today, my hair almost stands up on ends because she was the meanest human being I had ever met in my whole life. Myrtle had a boarding house and she ran it with an iron fist and with a reign of terror. She would bark out commands like a sergeant. If you did not move when she spoke she would scream and threaten you. She would get angry over the smallest details. When she went on the warpath, everyone would move out of the house. For anyone that messed with her, she would call the "law" and the law would come...and put them in jail.

Now we're in a new neighborhood and a new place. The name of the elementary school was William Randolph and I was in grade four. Ronnie was in grade two and Eleanor is in grade six. I had failed a grade and when someone asked me what grade I was in, I told them grade five. We were in a new neighborhood and I was used to fighting every day again. To get beat up didn't mean anything to me anymore. I would just fight. When we'd go out on the playground to play, kids would shove each other around. So, I cleaned up the playground. Everybody talked about this boy from Brooklyn who was real tough. So the boys in the school arranged a fight for me to fight with the toughest guy in school. We planned to fight after school hours at an abandoned gas station in the garage. The guy was named Jimmy and the boys were all talking to both of us. For some reason that day, I felt very strong and I beat that guy real bad.

I didn't grow very much from the fifth grade to the sixth grade but the other boys did. So, when I got in the sixth grade, I changed my whole image. I didn't want any more fighting. I was now "Billy Comfort" and I wasn't a bad boy who wanted to fight. Instead, I was a cheat. I got a reputation as being a very smart boy but actually, I was dumb. I cheated and made some of the best grades in my class.

By then Ronnie and I had gotten into singing, and Dad was always pushing us forward. Square dancing was popular. I learned the steps and was part of the lead couple. I became the caller of our square dance team and we competed with other schools by traveling and going all over western North Carolina. The schools would have competitions, and square dancing was as big as basketball or football. It was that important in that area. Eleanor did much better when we moved to Asheville. She made friends at school and was well liked. She danced on the "square dance team". This meant that you were with the "in crowd".

Anyway, I graduated from the sixth grade. By then my dad had a fight with Myrtle Robinson and he punched her out one day. She said that she was gonna call the law on him, so he ripped the telephone wire right out of the socket. We got out of there and found an apartment on Walnut Street.

In those days Asheville, NC was known as little San Francisco, and it was the center of drug trade in the area. At that time drugs had not gotten down to children as they have today; but adults were really into drugs, especially by injection. Asheville was also well known for being the center for bootlegging whiskey. Right underneath us was a man by the name of Joe Eaton who had a diner, and it was a place where men would come to eat. However, it was also a cover up for bootlegging. Ronnie gained their favor and he would go down and sing a song for them, and they would give him money.

Ronnie was making money by singing, and I made money also by shining shoes and selling papers. I bought all of my own clothes and personal items. We got into baseball and ping pong during the summer, and I got up a team. We won the city league and we were the champions. I was a second baseman and I was a leadoff man. I developed a way that when the ball was thrown right down the middle of the plate, I would step into the ball. When it came over the middle, because of my stance it would be "a ball". I learned how to get walks and also to turn my body in order to get hit with the ball and to steal bases. I was a terror around the bases; I would drive the pitchers crazy. All we knew was how to win, even though we weren't very good. We only lost one game all year, and that was when we played the all stars. So we got into ping pong, and in my age division, I became the ping pong champion of the city. My hand was quick, I was short and I was just good. I became the captain of the cheerleading squad, and there were three men on the squad. I became the captain of our square dance team and Ronnie followed suit. Ronnie and I sang over the radio, I sang with the Blue Ridge Boys and Ronnie sang with other Hillbilly Bands. We sang before different clubs and at schools when they held assemblies. We had a wonderful life in Asheville, NC.

Chapter 7

Then all of a sudden, my whole life went up in smoke. Here is how it suddenly happened! I'm sixteen now and I'm soon turning seventeen. An event took place that changed the rest of my life. I had been working as a delivery boy in a drugstore and it was Sunday. I had worked all day and I'm peddling my bicycle on my way home. I was half a block away from home and my father drove up in this big blue Hudson, and Ronnie is with him. He rolls down the window and he said, "Billy, Roxie and I have just had a fight. Are you coming with me, or are you staying with her?" I had to make a choice. My whole life was just half a block away - my clothing, shoes and all the things that were so important to me. I had even bought the bicycle I was riding on...but I saw Ronnie sitting in the back and I said, "Dad, I'm coming with you." He said, "Alright Billy, get off the bike, leave it there and get in the car. We're going to Elmira, NY."

So we drove 600 miles to Elmira, and my dad couldn't wait to get back to the bars and to his buddies. The first thing that he did was find a bar on Main Street where he used to hang out, and all of the old guys were still there. They didn't really care about him and we had no place to live, so we go to live with his aunt. I had come to love

Asheville; it was home to me. Now, in Elmira, Dad was having problems finding work, and he had the problem of knowing what to do with us. So, one day he said, "Billy you need to quit school and get a job." I'm in the eleventh grade, so I said, "Okay, I'll quit and get a job." The next day he said, "Billy, don't quit school; stay in school." Then later he says, "Billy, quit school and go in the service"; so I said, "Okay, Daddy." He changed his mind so many times and it was so confusing that I finally said, "It's time for me to get out."

 Chapter 8

Now I'm 17, the Korean War is on, I'm just 5'6" and I weigh about 122 lbs. I went to the recruiting office and took the exam. I scored low on everything but OJT Cook; this was another way of saying permanent KP. I took my basic training at Sampson Air Force Base, Geneva, NY.

Earlier along the way, we had gone to a Baptist church while in Asheville, NC. Roxie was a Baptist and Dad was a Protestant, so I had learned to fear God. I also learned from the Roman Catholics and was afraid of going to hell. Both denominations reinforced this teaching, and I am grateful that happened. I'm a little skinny kid in the military, and I'm in here with all these big guys going on through basic training. It's winter as I go in on December 2nd and snow is on the ground. The next year in February of 1952, I shipped out to Panama City, Florida, to Tyndale Air Force Base.

I felt before I went into the service that I was a sinner, and after I got into the service I was with all kinds of guys. There were gang members, druggies, womanizers, and offenders of all kinds. Everyday there were three subjects discussed - sex, money and alcohol. These were fellows that were so mixed up and had gotten into real trouble in their lives. They had been given the option of military service or jail time, and they chose the military. I was placed in the 3625th Food Service Squadron, as an OJT cook. So we worked long hours on a rotation basis, getting up at 2:00 am and walking a long distance to the mess hall. We had breakfast prepared by 4:00 am and the day was finished by 2:00 pm. We walked back to our squadron. The next day we'd be there at 8:00 a.m., and we'd be there until about 7:00 pm. The following day we were off.

I got involved in the base chapel, as I found it was the only place that I could get solitude. I also got involved in basketball and I got pretty good. My mind had degenerated and I got involved in some low life things too, but I don't really want to talk about them. One Saturday night, I opted to go into town with a friend named Lenny who was going to be shipped out. He is from Philly and he's a real nice fellow. We didn't have anything to do but walk up and down the street. At the end of the road was a boat dock where we noticed that they were selling fish. Then we looked over to our left and there wass an open lot, and people are coming into that lot now. So with nothing more to do, we go over to see what is happening. People are parking and getting out of their cars. Some had lawn chairs and in the center was a platform, a piano and a podium so we sat on the grass.

A lady comes up and plays an accordion and she begins to sing a song titled, "The Love of God". *"The love of God is greater far than tongue or pen can ever tell; it goes beyond the highest star and reaches to the lowest hell."* Finally, she said, *"If all this earth would pass away, there would always be the love of God."* I had no defenses up. I was completely open to what I heard because I didn't know it would be a religious meeting. Once she began singing about the love of God, I began thinking about God's love. Then a man got up and he began to preach. Before he began his sermon, he prefaced it with this remark, *"If there is anyone here tonight that would like to be saved after this service is over, we'd like for you to come forward after the service."*

I thought to myself, "Maybe this guy can help me." He preached a very powerful message, and when he finished my friend Lenny said, "Let's go." I said, " No, I'm gonna go down to see what this guy has to say." So, suddenly I walked to the platform and I stood there. The evangelist came over and as he looked at me, he said, "Hello". I said, "Sir, I want to be saved." I was a cool cat with a turned up collar, tight pants on and loud colored shoes, so I'm sure that my appearance revealed my need for salvation. He said, "Do you mean that, son?" I said, "Sir, I really do." He invited a group of men to come and he said, "Fellows, this boy would like to be saved." They took me aside by the platform and they all got down on their knees and they began to pray for me.

This was an Assembly of God meeting and I was on my knees right in the middle. They kept praying for me and

I thought, "I need to pray for myself." So, I did. I prayed, "Our Father which art in heaven, hallowed be thy name." I said, "No, that's not gonna work." So, I said, "Now I lay me down to sleep, I pray the Lord my soul to keep. If I should die before I wake, I ..." "No, no...that's not what I need to pray." "God is great and God is good and I thank Him...." "Hail Mary, mother of ..."

I said, "No...no, that's not it." Finally, a man who was in back of me placed his hands on my shoulder and said, "Son, say Jesus save me." I thought, "Oh, that's not hard." I opened my mouth and I was gonna say, "Jesus save me", but I couldn't say it. It was like the words were stuck and wouldn't come out; and all of a sudden, I envisioned myself in hell flames. I kept reaching for someone to pull me out of the flames, and I did something that I hadn't ever done in my whole life. I gave up completely the idea of ever becoming anything different than what I was. Any desires to accomplish anything in life were given up that day.

 Chapter 9

I knew that my mind was polluted; I knew my life was filled with darkness. When I gave up, suddenly Jesus appeared to me, and I saw Him dying on the cross for me. He looked so big and I looked so little; and I saw His love for me and I saw myself at the foot of the cross. My sins were so great. I didn't *say*, "Jesus save me." I began to scream it at the top of my voice. I begged Him to save me. I pleaded with Him to save me. All of a sudden, I felt something evil that had been in my body since I was a little boy, and it left my body that day. I repented of my sins and begged Jesus to save me, and He did. A glorious light flooded my heart and I got off my knees and said, "This stuff really works." I went back to my buddy and he said, "Bill, did you go to confession?" I said, "It was something like that, but I can't explain it."

When I got up off my knees, I was bigger than all of Tyndale Air Force Base. I had injured my back previously and was out of the kitchen, assigned to the barracks. I began reading the Bible and for the first time in my life, it made sense. As I read Genesis, "...and God said it was good," I thought, "Boy....it was good!" I spent lots of time reading the Bible. Then, something happened in my mind. I got so that I could talk to anybody: it didn't matter if it was an officer or whomever. I kept reading the Bible and my "gods" began to fall.

Basketball had been my god. I remember after I was saved, a buddy came over and he wanted to play basketball. I told him, "I think I'm gonna stay here and do a little reading." I mentioned earlier how dumb I was, what a cheat I was, what a low life I was and what a vulgar mouth I had. You know after Jesus saved me, vulgarity was gone; it came out only one time after that and I told my buddy that I would never say that again.

I heard if you went to the Tyndale Air Force Base Education Department and took this test, you could be recognized as a high school graduate. I had no prior time to study for it, but I went in and I prayed before the test. Whatever came to me, I wrote down. When the score was computed, I made all fours and fives on all my tests. My grades came back to the squadron area and they said, "Wow...we have to give you this job in the orderly room." I got a job as an administrative assistant, and they sent me to typing school where I got a grade of 95%.

I started going to church with a group of guys. We attended the Cove Baptist Church, and I became the adult teacher of the airman's class on the base. They made me the Assistant Sunday School Superintendent, but I wasn't getting any food for my soul. I started going to Youth for Christ on Saturday nights, and I would take some of my buddies with me. Many of them were saved. Then we started going to the jails. I led my first soul to Christ when I was saved for only six months. His name was George Jones and he was in jail. I had a ten day furlough and I got paid $82.00. I went down to the jail to see George and he said, "Billy, can you pay my bail and get me out." It was $25.00 and he got out. We both went over to the bus station and he said the next time the police come around, he would go back to jail. He asked me to buy him a ticket to get out to town and I bought it.

 Chapter 10

At that time my family had moved back to Asheville. When I got to Asheville, I was walking past the bus station going uptown; and I prayed and said, "Lord Jesus, help me to overcome this sinful town." I witnessed to my brother and my parents, and met some wonderful Christian people. Then I came back to the base.

I did so well on my job that I kept getting commendations. This was a turning point in my early Christian life. I began witnessing all over the place to all kinds of men; it didn't matter who they were. One day I was in the orderly room and it was very hot. I looked into the Commanding Officer's office, and he was perspiring profusely. My heart started beating rapidly. I thought what if Major Jolly goes to hell.

I couldn't stand to think about it, so I went into a stall in the bathroom, and I prayed because I knew I had to witness to him. I came out and went to his door. Major Jolly said, "Yessss!" I said, "Sir, may I speak with you?" He said, "Come on in son." I was so nervous, I didn't even report. He said, "Sit down son. What's on your mind?" I said, "Sir...I don't know if you've noticed before but I'm a Christian and I was wondering if you are a Christian too."

He said, "Son, I've been that way for a long time." He said, "Is there anything else that you wanted?" I said, "No sir." He said, "Dismissed!" I went out of the office. I didn't do a very good job of witnessing to him. In the course of witnessing to others, it had gotten out that I had been in the office with the old man; and that I had the old man on his knees begging for mercy.

When I would go to chow, even though usually there was lots of loud talking and so forth; when I arrived everything got deathly silent. I would get tracts from the chapel and would give everybody that was standing in line a tract. Finally, I was kicked out of the outfit and was sent to the 3627th Field Maintenance Squadron, where I became a mail clerk. I used the mail clerk office as a way to give out tracts to all of the men that were getting mail. I witnessed to everyone that walked. I had a very good relationship with the chaplains, Major Wills and Major Wiley, who treated me like a son. When I'd get off in my emphasis, they would help me.

 Chapter 11

The Korean War ended in 1953, and I heard if you were in a non-critical career field, that you could get an early out. I had put in two full years, so I put in for an early discharge. All of the people who were involved in my life signed off on my discharge. They thought it would be good for me to go to school and study for the ministry. (I think they wanted to get rid of me.) I got out of the Air Force, and that very day I went to Cove Baptist Church and spoke to Pastor Hugh Pyle about going to Bob Jones University to study for the ministry. So he said, "Billy, I think we should give you a license to preach." On December 29th, 1953, I received a license to preach from Cove Baptist Church. When I went home, I had a whole month at home and I spent an hour in prayer every day. I led some people to the Lord. I led a boy named Kermit to the Lord and he bowed his head right there on his bicycle; and when he lifted his head, you could see that he was different.

When I arrived on the Bob Jones University Campus, they took me to Smith's dormitory. While standing out in front of that building, the Holy Spirit touched me in a special way. The new people always had the opportunity to give a testimony and this fellow gave his testimony, and it was really powerful. His name was Keith, and we became soul brothers; and we would go down to the lake, where we would pray together. He had been a buck sergeant, and had been all state football in Minnesota. There was an extension group of preacher boys; there were a thousand of them when we were there. We would go to hospitals and rescue missions and so forth, and witness. There was a group called the Columbian extension group and I was invited to go with them. The man who was leading it made a few mistakes and the proprietor of the beer garden called the college and they demoted him.

My friend Al Bradshaw had the leadership for a while but he didn't want to do it. "Al" had been an all star hockey player in Canada, he was Canadian. He was an incredible athlete and was also tremendous in hockey. After a month, Al asked me to take over the group. I was only 19 and I was one of the smallest guys in the group. We would get four or five carloads of guys and we'd go down to witness on the street. There was a Servicemen's Center and we'd invite the men to come into the Serviceman's Center. There was also a rescue mission on Oliver Street. As time progressed, there were some hardcore Christians in our group; and when we hit the streets of Columbia, SC., things began to happen. Keith would pray for me all week and I would pray for Keith all week. At the end of Saturday, there were a hundred service men that had accepted Christ.

The highlight of the evening was a gospel meeting and I would always give my testimony. I'd tell them how I got saved while I was in the service and I would give the invitation; and often many of them made professions of faith in Christ. I led this group as long as I was on campus. I heard that if you read Luke chapter sixteen every day, that you would get such a passion for souls that you would be more fruitful in witnessing. Every day I had my devotions that included Luke 16. When I gave my testimony, I always spoke about the rich man and Lazarus; Hell was on my mind all of time. When I was in a room of people, all I could think about was, "They're going to hell.... they're going to hell."

I would go to bed at night and during my sleep I'd wake up my roommate because I would be crying, "They're going to hell...they're going to hell!" So, I had a goal to lead one soul to Christ each day. In my junior year I had the privilege to go off campus anytime I wanted to, so every day I was on the street and I wouldn't come back until someone had prayed for salvation.

 Chapter 12

During the summer, I returned to Elmira, NY. By this time, my family was living in Elmira and I began witnessing on the street. Some of the students from Bob Jones University were from Elmira, New York and they also attended Birchwood Baptist Tabernacle in Elmira Heights. The church had a very large youth group and they also had a Sunday afternoon radio program which the young people ran. Shirley Evans read the poetry. I knew when I met her that I would one day marry her. She did not know this because we really did not have that much fellowship together. She had her heart set on the foreign mission field, and I was single minded with one great passion and that was to win souls to Christ. I kept her deep down in my soul and her image locked in. Well, she went to London Bible Institute in Ontario, Canada to study to be a foreign missionary to Africa.

I went back to Bob Jones University in Greenville, South Carolina to resume studying for the ministry. During the second summer I went to Mount Airy, North Carolina and went door to door as a Bible Salesman. We went to a church called White Plains Baptist Church and I had a good summer there.

The third summer, there was a man at Birchwood Baptist Church who was a missionary to Honduras whose name was Robert Howell. Robert Howell invited Cliff Proper and me to come down and preach for him. So Cliff Proper, a school mate, and I scraped up enough money to fly out of Miami FL, to the Honduras. We went to the Republic of Honduras and preached down there all summer. I hitchhiked to Miami, Florida. Someone told me about a missionary rest home in Miami that served missionaries coming and going to the mission field. The director picked me up from a telephone booth, and later Cliff was picked up. We didn't know we would be at the same home. We had a wonderful summer in Honduras and led many to the Lord. We went to Utila Island, and a blind man named Jonathan James lived there. Many went blind there because they were watermen and they used a magnifying glass to see the fish. They lost their sight because the sun would shine on the glass. I led Jonathan and his wife to Christ.

We also went out to Utila Cays and we preached there; then we went to the Island of Roatan. While there, I picked up amoebic dysentery and became deathly sick. We went over to La Ceiba on the mainland. I had so many amoebae in my body, I could see them swimming in the toilet. A missionary there paid for me to go to the hospital to get treatment. When the summer was over, I was a walking skeleton. I hitchhiked 1800 miles from Miami back to our home in Elmira, and then I had to go back to Bob Jones University. That was my junior year and I was sick all of that year. Such darkness came into me during this period, but I had such a strong will. If someone said read five chapters a day, I'd read ten. If they said memorize a verse, I memorized the whole chapter. If they said memorize a chapter, I'd memorize the whole book.

During that year, I was very sick and I'd go into the bathroom and cry every day. My heart and mind were filled with so much darkness, I was depressed; but I continued to witness and lead people to Christ. But in my room I struggled and I prayed, "Oh God, you know how hard I'm trying." Finally, Keith Davey was connected with a group called Christian Service Centers, Inc. where the director was E. W. Crockett. Keith told Crockett about me. He opened up the door for my last year to go to San Antonio, T.X. I hitchhiked 60 hours to get there. First I went home, and my dad told me not to hitchhike in N.Y. because they would take me to jail.

 Chapter 18

When I arrived in San Antonio, I got there on a Monday. They had expected me earlier. Crockett was disappointed that I didn't arrive on time, but we worked that out. I witnessed to many people that summer. This was another turning point in my life. There was a lady named Lillian Bivings and she told me that she knew a man in Houston, Texas that she wanted me to meet. His name was Pastor Bob Thieme. A friend of mine had been with this man about a year earlier, so I was willing to go meet him. We arrived early and had a meal, and then I witnessed to a few people.

That evening, I met Bob and he talked to me about carnality, spirituality, the indwelling of Christ, resting in Christ and not struggling. His words were way over my head; I wasn't getting it. He gave me a book called, "What is Spirituality?" The next thing I knew I was transformed in a way that I had never been before. I didn't have to "find" the Lord, He was always there; and this book helped me to rest in His words. I went back to the campus and began passing Bob's book out on the campus, but was soon called in on the carpet. I had made some stupid mistakes and I was in trouble with the campus. I was scheduled to be in

"Who's Who", but they took all of my accomplishments away from me.

So, I went into hiding on the campus and I became low key. I knew I was on the verge of them kicking me out. They were very good to me and I don't fault them for what they did. They were the authorities, and I had taken the leadership position without consulting them, and that was wrong. The school administration had also taken the leadership of the Columbia Extension Group away from me; but then the Extension Group began falling apart. When the administrator saw that I had been in mourning and was repentant, they asked me to take over the group again. They said that the men wanted me to lead them. I graduated at the end of that year. When I graduated, Bob Jones Gospel Fellowship ordained me and I was back in the good graces of the University.

I went out to San Antonio and worked with Christian Service Centers, Inc., on North Alamo Street, right around the corner from Travis Street. I had my Greek New Testament and I fell in love with it. My job was to take care of the third floor; I had a desk and a room and used my time to translate the Greek New Testament. As time progressed, some Christian men came to us and said that we should go to Norfolk, VA. It was the home of the Sixth Fleet and it's a NATO port where there are men coming in from all over the world. We decided to go to Norfolk and we secured lodging; there were six of us. We walked the street for five or six days and led many to

Christ, and we felt that God had called us to Norfolk. It was decided that I should move to Norfolk and help start a Service Center there.

The area where we were to open the Christian Servicemen's Center was filled with prostitution, bars and gambling joints; and we were right in the middle of it all. The word got out that if you go to that Serviceman Center, they're gonna preach to you; so many of them wouldn't come. But we noticed that there were men who had come and they were staying and we felt led to train them. Keith Davey, Bob Walker and Billy Comfort were the men heading up this Servicemen's Center. My job was to keep things clean, teach the Bible class and to witness.

 Chapter 14

So, here I wound up in Norfolk, VA working in a Servicemen's Center; and in the meanwhile Shirley Evans was teaching school in the Christian School of Greater Fall River, Massachusetts. Five years passed and I began thinking about Shirley, so I wrote to her pastor, Clyde Truax, for her address. We began writing to each other and her letters were wonderful. Then one day she invited me to come up and visit. I went up to see her and purposed in my heart that I would not hold her hand or kiss her. I wanted our relationship to be above board. We had a heart to heart talk and concluded that we would continue to write and see where the Lord would take the relationship.

We later went to Tiverton, RI for the Thanksgiving holiday; where we spent the day together and it was there that I told her that I loved her. She came down to Norfolk, VA, during the 1959 Christmas holidays. It was on Christmas Eve that I gave her the engagement ring, and we were married February 5, 1960.

For the next two years both Shirley and I worked in the Christian Servicemen's Center where we won servicemen to Christ and then was able to disciple those that were stationed in the area. Many men, upon being discharged, went to Bible College to study for the ministry. It was at this time when our oldest son Derrick Mark Comfort was born. The hours Shirley and I were working prohibited us from having any family life whatsoever. I felt as though my 9 ½ years of working with servicemen were coming to a closure.

Chapter 15

Then suddenly a door opened in Chesapeake, VA and I was given a call to pastor our first church at age 28. The church was the Victory Baptist Church, at 1200 Kempsville Road, Chesapeake, VA. We fell in love with the people and they loved us.

It was at this time when Paul William Comfort, our second son, was born. For the next 6 ½ years we worked night and day winning people to Christ, baptizing them and training them to be a witness for Christ. Our church grew from a handful of people to a vibrant evangelistic church. We normally worked 80 hours a week to keep the momentum rolling. Eventually I worked myself so hard that I began having violent head and stomach aches. They kept getting more intense until I had to resign in order to get my health back. It was one of our most difficult decisions but Shirley and I both knew that we needed a change.

Our next assignment took place at the large Alexander Baptist Church, at 3801 Turnpike Road, Portsmouth VA in January 1968. The pastor H. L. Tolbert needed a minister of education, and hired me to win and reach people for Christ. He took me out to the Alexander Park Housing

District and showed me the hundreds of homes within a half block of the church. Then he showed me the three buses that the church used to pick up people. He said, "Well, Billy, I want you to fill up those buses with people." The first Sunday we had 29 people that rode in three buses. One year later there were 254 people that rode in five buses. My goal was to knock on 100 doors each week and win many people to Christ. The Sunday school enrollment had been 950 but when we moved on to our next assignment the enrollment climbed to 1385. We would baptize 100 people a year, and lead the Portsmouth Baptist Association in growth while I was at Alexander Baptist Church.

The highlight of the year was the church Sunday School Training Convention which was taught by Rev. Charles Barnes, from the Maryland Baptist Convention. Charles and I became good friends and he told me that he felt that I could be a help in Maryland. By then, I'd gotten my health back and was ready to begin again my duties as the Senior Pastor of a church. Well, this led to our coming to Maryland in 1971 to pastor the Kettering Baptist Chapel in Largo, MD. The chapel met at the Kettering Elementary School on Sunday mornings, with a membership of 22 people. Again, we dug in our heels and determined to visit the many homes in the area and lead as many people to Christ as possible. Two and a half years later the membership had grown to 150 and we had a brand new beautiful building.

In the meanwhile, I was studying for my first Master of Arts Degree at the Capital Bible Seminary, Lanham MD. The schedule was great as I was able to take a few courses in the morning and then begin visiting in the afternoon. I was just ready to graduate when another sudden occurrence took place in our lives. Much to our surprise, several people in the Kettering Baptist Church felt like that the church needed a new pastor to give the church a better chance of growth. My last official act as pastor of Kettering Baptist Church was to dedicate the new building.

So in 1974, we then received a call to pastor The First Baptist Church of Eastport, on Chesapeake Avenue, Annapolis MD. Little did we know then, this was God's perfect will for our lives because He had a much larger purpose which was waiting for us in Annapolis MD. No one can ever kick you out, they only kick you up! The next year, I did graduate from Capital Bible Seminary with a Master of Arts Degree in Biblical Studies. I was also able to begin an Extension School for Washington Bible College in our large Education Room at the First Baptist Church.

 Chapter 16

Here is how this much larger purpose for our lives unfolded. I had very large office and the church was about a half block of real estate. A man named Bob Wright came to the door one day. Bob had been a Lt. Commander in the Navy and he became a special friend to me. We talked about the Campus Life Crusade of reaching your community for Christ. Before we finished we were talking about the church government and Bob told me that what I was saying was how his church was set up; and that he was the "overseer" of about four churches. So, Bob and Mary Jane, his wife invited Shirley and me out to lunch. While we talked, he invited me to become a part of New Covenant Churches. We went to the first meeting and it blew me away. In all of my life I had never seen so much humility and so much deferring to the other person, with nobody trying to be a big shot. We had communion and it was so wonderful.

I had married a couple while living in Kettering; and they moved to the Eastern Shore of Maryland. When they found out that I was pastor of the First Baptist Church of East Port; they visited me and told me how God was working in their lives, and how they had dedicated their lives to Christ. They invited Shirley and me to a Bible study and it was Labor Day weekend. (We were then in the 70's. I graduated in 1975 and this year was 1975.) Shirley and I went to their home and we went to a neighbor's home for a picnic at a large piece of property, owned by Dr. Donald Novak. When we arrived, they treated us so warmly; it was similar to the reception we received at the New Covenant meeting. These people hugged each other and Shirley visited the women inside the home and I stayed outside and played ball with the young guys. (Baseball, football and basketball) I had long endurance and could play all day.

Finally, I went inside. They were having an interdenominational Bible study and they invited me to join them. They had many questions as they studied and I could answer them, so they invited me to become the Bible teacher. I told Shirley, after we left, that this was all wrong; those people should go to their own churches. When I went back to my church, I couldn't help but remember how loving and wonderful these people were. I found myself being drawn to them when I had time free on Friday nights. So, I became their Bible teacher and finally, I felt led of God to step out in faith to start a church on the Eastern Shore.

I was getting ready to resign from First Baptist Church of East Port in December. On Friday nights, we had a group of 60 people at the Bible study. I asked the Lord to show me His will by giving five families that would commit themselves to starting a new church. When we counted the number of committed families there were four plus our family which made five. So we resigned the pastorate at the First Baptist Church of Eastport and moved back to our home in Kettering in December of 1976. Thus, 14 years as a Baptist pastor came to a close.

I had rented our home in Kettering out when we left for Annapolis, and moving back into our home we were surprised to discover that it needed many repairs. But the men of New Covenant Church came over and used their own money and time, and re-furbished the home; it was like brand new. (They sanded the floors, painted the walls and put in new sheet rock where it had been broken with holes in the walls.) We sold this home and moved to Chesapeake Avenue in Kentmorr on Kent Island, Stevensville, MD.

I moved into our new home in Kentmorr in February 1977. Later, Shirley and the boys moved to Queen Anne's County in May 1977. Shirley and my sons stayed in Kettering until the boys were out of school. I had only been in Kentmorr for a little over a month when a father of one of the families came to me and told me that he wasn't happy with the church and that he was leaving.

The county was closed to any new churches at that time. I founded the "New Covenant Church" and I was immediately suspected. There were few churches and they had been there for years. They didn't like anything that was new and they were not open to new people. We became suspects and there were many stories told about me. I made up my mind that they would have to like me. Things got so bad I thought they would throw us out into Chesapeake Bay but we lived down all of the rumors and fears and we served the community. Our family was weary of having to move every two or three years and we believed that it was time for us to finally get planted on the Eastern Shore of Maryland. Little did we know then what it was going to cost! We wound up in a 17 year war with the state, county, and town. It all had to do with religious freedom. You can fight for religious freedom from the outside or better yet why not get on the inside? The Comfort family became totally involved in the community.

The Lord gave us strong leaders and some of the existing churches saw us as an outsider who was a threat. But we made up our mind that they were going to like us whether they wanted to or not. Eventually, they knew that we were here to stay and the suspicions left.

 Chapter 17

The Lord opened the door for us to purchase a building that had been a historical landmark in Queenstown, in Queen Anne's county. (It was the original building called Queenstown Elementary School). Earlier that year, I was in a presbytery meeting with New Covenant Church pastors. I began to tell the pastors that we had young men with lots of zeal but they didn't know Bible doctrine; they were not grounded in the Word. They asked me what I recommended, so I told them that we needed to teach them. We had a long and heated discussion, but finally Bob Wright said that we needed to start a Bible Institute. They asked me to be the director. So, we started a Bible Institute and it was called New Life Bible Institute at 804 Windsor Road, Arnold, MD. The New Covenant Churches had just bought the church on Windsor Road. The location was a perfect central location where we were able to attract 15 cooperating churches.

Therefore, we started out there in January 1977, and 15 churches cooperated. In the process of time, we had over 1,200 people that had taken courses and become leaders. There were some pastors, elders, deacons and different workers in the church; but we couldn't give degrees. At this time, our church on the Eastern Shore was growing and we were attracting people that were hardcore Christians, who wanted to be like first century Christians. Things were going well and I always had the presbytery to support me. If we had a problem in the church, they would come over and adjudicate. Whatever their decision, we had to abide by it. We had some problems and I called them, but we resolved the problems before they arrived. However, they did come anyway and they reinforced me as the leader. That was so wonderful to have that type of support.

 Chapter 18

Our church began a Christian Academy in 1982. All of a sudden, we were informed that we could go to jail for having a Christian Academy without the state completely controlling all aspects of the curriculum. It so happened that three different Maryland state departments had proposed legislation which gave them authority to determine what, when, who, and how education was to be administered in church schools. Therefore, we had no choice but to get involved in fighting back.

When the hearings took place in the Maryland State Chambers there were so many church leaders present in opposition to the bill that it died right on the floor of the Senate Hearings Chambers. That was the beginning, or you might say, "round one" in our fight for religious freedom. So New Covenant Churches became very active on the political scene. We were pro-life and we felt like Christians needed a voice in the community and in the legislation. At first, I was adverse to the idea but after a while I was convinced that I either had to do it or get out of New Covenant Churches which I loved so much. I came, dragging my heels at the start.

This was another life changing event for me. Here's what happened: my youngest son Paul, at age 16 had gone down to the House of Delegates in Annapolis, the capital of Maryland. He began talking with the district delegates about Christian issues. The delegates really felt like Paul was too young and didn't know what he was talking about. Actually, one delegate showed Paul out of his office. When Paul came home, he and Derrick talked until 4:00 a.m., since they were sleeping in the same room. Paul told Derrick, "You are 21 and you can run for the House of Delegates."

Well, Derrick had just come back from Officer's Candidate School, in Fort Benning, GA and he was now a Second Lieutenant in the National Guard. He had been the Distinguished Honor Graduate of 180 men at Ft. Benning, GA, and he was only 21 years of age. Paul told him that he would be his campaign manager. We were in a district where the people were very settled into traditions, and Democrats were very powerful. We were Republicans. So Derrick said, "Let's talk to Dad and if he goes for it, I'll do it." So we took on five counties on the Eastern Shore: Queen Anne, parts of Caroline, Talbot, Kent and Cecil Counties.

My job was to go to the churches, and many people in our churches got into the campaign. We waged a fierce campaign. Our opponents tore down our signs but we would come back and put them up. In the middle of the campaign, I introduced myself to the Democrat candidate that we were running against, and we became very good friends. He told me that he had had the same convictions as we did, and that if he won, that he would honor those convictions. He told me that he was a man of his words and it proved to be true. He had the most conservative voting record in the whole state. We also became friends with Senator Walter Baker. They told me that any time we were in Annapolis and I needed a desk, that I could use theirs if they were out of the office. So we had a wonderful relationship. Even though Derrick lost the election, the issues that he stood for won the day!

In 1986 Derrick ran and won the chairmanship of the Queen Anne's County Republican Party Central Committee. Derrick had turned his attention to the Army National Guard. He became the Company Commander of Queen Anne's County Armory in 1984 and was promoted to Captain in 1986. He was offered a position in the White House which he declined to accept because it was a 7:00 a.m. – 7:00 p.m. job.

We were not one sided in our outreach because that same year Paul Comfort was elected to the Democratic Central Committee. Paul also got onto WCTR AM radio with a news and information show. In 1984 he was elected as president of the Governor's Youth Advisory Council. In 1985 he was elected president of Queen Anne's County Young Democrats. So we were able to influence both political parties.

Shirley Comfort became the Director of "Eastern Shore of Maryland for Concerned Women for America" which she served from 1980-1984. She was appointed to the Queen Anne's County Board of Election as Supervisor and served from 1987-1993. Shirley was given a White House Security Clearance where she would read the president's mail. She also became the president of the Queen Anne's County Republican Women's Party.

I focused my skills in journalism from 1986 on and became a columnist for the Record Observer/Bay Times and The Banner. My column was called "The Bible Says." Through this medium I was able to promote solid biblical truths. I was appointed to Queen Anne's County Commission on Aging from 1985-1989 and served as vice chairman, and then as chairman. I later became involved in a Queenstown zoning dispute which threatened to zone our church out of existence. So in 1990 I was appointed to the Queenstown Planning Commission and served as the recording secretary for the next three years.

Paul went through college on scholarships that he earned and became a leader on campus at Chesapeake College, in Wye Mills, MD, where he was elected president of the student body. He was also used of God at the University of Maryland. He discovered that the place of power was on the radio, and he had a radio program called "The Rock That Doesn't Roll". He played Christian music all the way through the program and he graduated with honors.

 Chapter 19

In 1984 I was on my knees in prayer and I looked down through the future of New Covenant Bible Institute. I realized that it would never go as far as desired without someone getting a doctorate degree. I kept looking over my shoulders for someone to go to graduate school. I fasted and prayed for four days and nights, and was finally led to go for my doctorate.

I had a friend that had become the Academic Vice President of Oxford Graduate School in Dayton, TN. I called him and was accepted as a student in 1984, even though I didn't have money. We started an academy in our church and had a wonderful group of students. They had a bake sale and earned $2,000; and the leaders in the Academy and the student body gave me $1,000. Many of the pastors and other church leaders in the churches gave money and others gave me free flying miles to make the trip to TN, when needed. My whole doctorate program was paid for by the pastors of New Covenant Churches. Shirley and I had the honor of going to Oxford, England, and I studied at Oxford University and the Bodleian Library while there.

The year was 1985, and Shirley and I had just returned from Oxford University, in England. I was working on my Doctor of Philosophy Degree with Oxford

Graduate School, Dayton, Tennessee. Part of the program was to attend Oxford University and take lectures at the Department of External Studies.

Shirley discovered a lump in her breast and decided to forego surgery, radiation and chemotherapy. She determined to overcome her problem with nutrition. So we took all our money out of savings, and she went to Boston, MA, to the Hippocrates Health Institute. A lady in our church went with Shirley. She was there two weeks and learned their system. We grew our own sprouts and ate raw food for nine months. At the end of nine months the cancer lumps had totally disappeared.

This was a very difficult time in our lives. We were greatly tested in many ways. I was in a head-on-collision when my car slid on the ice and banged into a concrete wall; no one was hurt but the car needed to be repaired.

The note on our church came due, and we did not have the money to pay. A man wanted to help us buy the building, so I secured the services of an attorney. I asked the attorney for the deed and the papers, drove through a blizzard, went to Tuckahoe, NY and got the friend to loan us the money. I changed the oil in my car, and filled up a gas can so that I wouldn't have to stop for gas. Paul went with me. Cars were stranded along the road, so we got behind a tractor trailer and were able to arrive at our destination. I called the man at his home, and at 5:00 a.m. over coffee, the man signed the papers. He guaranteed that he would put up the money for our church. We thanked him and drove back. So, we were able to buy that building.

Problems arose in the congregation. This could have split the church. I was also taking a course in statistics as well as writing my dissertation. So many things were happening that I thought I'd lose my mind. Life did not stop.

I was chairman of the Commission on Aging, Vice President of New Covenant Churches, President of New Covenant Christian Academy and pastor of the church. But the most difficult thing during this period of time was the pressure that we received from our peers who wanted Shirley to receive chemotherapy and radiation. The pressure was so intense that I kept Shirley home when I went to the pastors/wives meetings. These were just a few of the trials, but greater is He who lives within than anything that life can throw at us.

My stepmother, Roxie, died of cancer. Roxie's death was a long drawn out thing. My father waited on her day and night. When she died, it was devastating to him.

Of course, my mother had gotten out of the mental institution in Long Island and had come to Elmira. My parents had no contact. My mom later married a man who forced his way into her life. She escaped from him by submitting herself to the Elmira Psychiatric Center. She eventually died there at age 81.

 Chapter 20

My wife and I lived on a very small wage for several years. I raised my boys on a salary of $300 per week. I refused to take a raise because that meant we would lose some of the teachers in the Academy. But God provided and we ate well and managed to live a healthy lifestyle.

I stayed at the church as pastor for 17 years, and I got my Doctorate of Philosophy in 1986. The state of Maryland passed a law which was sponsored by the delegation from our district. Senator Walter Baker, Clayton Mitchell who later became speaker of the House, Jack Ashley and Ron Guns voted that a church could have a college and grant religious degrees provided that they met certain criteria. That happened in 1986, and for three years I couldn't meet the criteria because so many things were happening in my life. But in 1989 the presbytery began telling me that I needed to get the paperwork done, and the rest is history.

The Maryland Higher Education Commission, on December 4, 1989, certified the New Covenant Christian College, which later became Chesapeake Bible College. We were certified as a religious degree granting institution as set forth in section 11-202 of the Education Article of the Annotated Code of Maryland. Our first graduating class was on June 30, 1991, with four men receiving the Bachelor of Ministry Degree. By October 27, 2007 over 1,000 graduates had received their degrees/diplomas from Chesapeake Bible College & Seminary. Mary Elizabeth Rogers, at age 80, was the 1001 graduate with the Doctor of Religious Education Degree.

There were many wonderful things that took place in the 1990s. Paul Comfort, our youngest son, matriculated in the University of Maryland Law School in 1992. He graduated in 1996 with the Jurist Doctorate of Law Degree and the Moot Court Champion of his class. Dr. Ron Comfort, my brother, founded Ambassador Baptist College in 1989 in Shelby NC. By 1997 this same college moved from Shelby, NC to a new campus in Lattimore, NC. Ron served this college as president for a total of 20 years.

I earned my second doctor's degree, which was the N.D. Degree in 1999 from Clayton College of Natural Health, Birmingham AL. The 1990s were also significant for both my wife Shirley and me. In 1993 I resigned as pastor of the New Covenant Church in Queenstown, MD because I felt it was time for me to devote my full time energy as President of Chesapeake Bible College & Seminary. The church agreed to support me full time until the college was financially able to assume that responsibility. The church appointed me to be the Apostle of the church whose main ministry was the presidency of

Chesapeake Bible College. The church fulfilled this responsibility for the next four years. So it was my joy to serve the New Covenant Church for a total of 21 years.

 Chapter 21

Things really began to come into focus by October of 1993. It so happened that Lorraine Evans, Shirley's mother, had major brain surgery and wanted to return to her four room apartment home at 10 Aspen Ridge, Elmira, NY. So Shirley and I decided to take a week off and visit her in Elmira. We would stay with her in her apartment home so that she could have the company that she needed. We had been there six days and were preparing the next day to come back to Maryland. There was, however, a large question that was before the Evans family. Who was going to take care of Mom Evans? We went to bed that night and the Lord kept me awake all night and shared with me a plan of how we could take care of Mom Evans. The next morning, Shirley said, "Oh honey, I can't describe it but I felt as though I was in a state of euphoria all night!" I said, "That is interesting, I could not sleep all night but the Lord wants us to take care of Mom, and here is how we will do it." The Lord instructed us to move to 10 Aspen Ridge, in Elmira, NY where Shirley could take care of her mother.

So in December of 1993, we left our home in Queenstown empty, scattered our furniture in five different locations and moved to Elmira in the dead of winter. The New Covenant Church blessed us and helped us to move.

This was another "suddenly" in our journey of faith. Shirley and I found ourselves in this small four room apartment. Her job was to care for Mom, and my job was to commute back and forth to Queenstown MD and in the meanwhile, travel throughout the continent promoting the College. My office was the trunk of our car, and the car was on the snow covered street.

Well, I ran into a problem because I had nowhere to park the car. When the snow plow came through, the car was immobilized. So I parked the car on the lot of a business across the street. The next day when I went to get the car, the business owner had graciously provided me with a flat tire. He told me to get the car off his lot or else. Some friends offered me an empty bedroom in their house to have an office. I parked the car in front of their house but the highway came through paving the road and I had to move the car. So I got permission from the grocery store owner to park on his lot, but later his wife left a threatening note on my windshield. She told me to get that "xxxxx" car off the lot or she would call the police. That was only one of the many challenges we faced.

The weather was also a challenge as I travelled promoting the college. For the next four years, my travels took me to Canada, New York, New Jersey, Connecticut, Pennsylvania, West Virginia, Georgia, and Jamaica. God gave us favor everywhere we went and He opened doors for the College to set up a network of Schools of Ministry. I drove on icy roads, through a flood, through a hail storm and on the back end of a hurricane without being hurt. I would drive to the College office in Queenstown and work around the clock.

Shirley and I had a little trailer which the Chesapeake Motors let us park on their property. Our friends Bob and Fran Bradshaw owned the property and insisted that we keep the trailer on their property. So after working long hours in the office, I would drive to the trailer and spend the night. Our son Derrick was able to sell our home on Dudley Avenue in Queenstown. So we put the money into a retirement fund.

The only way we were able to solve the Elmira parking problem was to buy our own home. The Lord opened the way that we were able to take some of our retirement money and purchase a home at 105 Oakwood Avenue, Elmira Heights, NY. It was while we lived there that Shirley founded the Office of External Studies for Chesapeake Bible College & Seminary.

We lived in this home for the next two years and then another "suddenly" happened. Mom grew worse and Shirley's sister, who is a licensed practical nurse, was the only family member with the skills to care for her. Shirley also became concerned about me travelling through the weather conditions, and she knew it was time for us to come back to the Eastern Shore of Maryland.

 Chapter 22

We were immediately challenged with another set of problems. They were two-fold in nature. The first problem was that the College had outgrown the two offices in the New Covenant Church of Queenstown. The second problem was that we needed another home to live in. Eventually, we located two acres of land on wooded property in Caroline County with a very large house on it. God led us to take out all of our retirement money and purchase the house. It was able to serve as a residence for Shirley and me, as well as office space for the College. Little did I dream then that leaders from all over the world would come to this out of the way location to connect with the Chesapeake Bible College & Seminary.

In the process of time, we built onto the building three times. This provided the space we needed for six college offices as well as a file room, a library, and lodging space for visitors. The Lord has given us a wonderful staff to work with. Debbie Rafter is the College Secretary and Treasurer. Ed Connatser is the College Registrar, as well as the Director of External Studies. Dr. Bob Rundall is the Dean of Academic Services. Erika Bixler is the Logistics Coordinator. Dr. Shirley Comfort serves as the Executive

Vice President and I, Dr. William Comfort, am the College President.

As the College began to develop, it was felt that we needed to deepen our foundations. We read in the New Testament that the New Jerusalem has foundations (Hebrews 11:10; Revelations 21:14). We needed to deepen the work as well as to expand it. God gave us seven very solid foundations to build the College upon. They are as follows:

(1) December 4, 1989 the College was certified by the Maryland Higher Education Committee to be a religious degree granting institution.

(2) April 23, 1996 the College was accredited by the Accrediting Commission International.

(3) May 29, 1997 the College was approved by the National Christian Counselors Association as an Affiliate College.

(4) August 22, 2006 the Mid Atlantic District of the International Pentecostal Holiness Church approved the College as their Regional Bible College.

(5) November 14, 2006 the College was incorporated in the state of Maryland. Prior to that time the College was a ministry of the Love Church of Maryland, Inc. Now it was a stand-alone organization.

(6) June 11, 2007 the Internal Revenue Service approved the College as a 501C Tax Deductible Organization.

(7) September 1, 2008 the Oxford Educational Network accredited Chesapeake Bible College & Seminary as a fully accredited and affiliated University.

As the foundations were being laid deeper and stronger, it was necessary also to expand the curriculum. The following represents some examples of the expanded curriculum:

>The Diploma of Ministry calls for 30 credits.

>The Associate of Christian Ministry Degree calls for 60 credits.

>The 3 Bachelor's Degrees each call for 120 credits, and are as follows:

    The Bachelor of Ministry Degree

    The Bachelor of Christian Ministry Degree

    The Bachelor of Religious Education

>There are 7 different Master's Degrees and most of them call for 48 credits advanced credits.

The Master's Degrees are as follows:

    Master of Biblical Counseling

    Master of Christian Counseling

    Master of Pastoral Counseling

    Master of Ministry

    Master of Christian Ministry

    Master of Religious Education

Master of Worship Ministry

Master of Theological Studies.

>The Doctor of Clinical Pastoral Degree calls for
65 credits.

>The Doctor of Religious Education Degree calls
for 65 credits.

>The Doctor of Theology Degree calls for 78
credits.

>The Doctor of Worship Degree calls for 56 credits.

John 15:1-8 and I Corinthians 12:12-27 afford us two tremendous examples of the Body of Christ. Both passages may be interpreted individually but they also have a larger corporate application. The Body of Christ is actually a network of church ministries extending all over the earth. The process of networking began for Chesapeake Bible College & Seminary in 1997. Pastor Victor Dunning was the pastor of the Hopewell Christian Fellowship in Elverson, PA. He opened the door for the College to network with the Charismatic Mennonite Network of Churches in Pennsylvania to which he was connected. So the next thing I knew we had Schools of Ministry in three of their churches.

Pastor Rick Farley was the Overseer of the Pentecostal Church of God in the Atlantic Region. God gave us favor with them and several of their churches opened their doors to Chesapeake Bible College & Seminary. These churches were in the Eastern United States as well as Canada and Jamaica. A short time later in

1998, Dr. Shirley and I attended a conference where Rodney Howard Browne was the speaker. It was held at the Victory Christian Center in New Castle, DE. This wonderful church, of which Dr. Gary Whetstone is the pastor, has the School of Biblical Studies. Eventually the Lord bonded us together where we began accepting their credits and enabled their students to earn degrees. Out of that arrangement came the Able Ministers International network, of which Drs. Wayne and Diane Hendrickson were the overseers. Their ministry is in the Ukraine where they start Bible Schools.

Next God networked us with The Interdenominational Bible Institute, of Camden, DE, with Dr. Samuel Dixon. The Master's Commission in Dagsboro, DE and the Ground Zero Master's Commission in New London, PA were also living links that we were able to tie into. The Holy Trinity Theological College and Seminary in Libertytown, MD formed a working agreement with us. Louisiana Baptist University in Shreveport, LA and Chesapeake Bible College & Seminary became allied together. The Mid Atlantic District of the Pentecostal Church of America extends over a very large area. Dr. Terry Bailey, Dr. Ron Carpenter and Bishop Wesley Russ paved the way for Chesapeake Bible College & Seminary to be received as the Mid Atlantic District Bible College. Drs. Phil Byler, Judy Byler, Cindy Byler and Tim Byler promoted Chesapeake Bible College in the State of Georgia. A great harvest of graduates generated from this network.

Pastor Scott Thompson, Director of Eternal Life Concepts, has an extensive ministry into the prisons of Florida. He paved the way for the Florida prisons to approve Chesapeake Bible College & Seminary for part of their Penal Institution Rehabilitation Program. The network eventually opened the door for the College to begin teaching Bible courses to the prisoners in Florida as well as Louisiana and Maryland. Saint Alcuin House Seminary, Blaine, MN, is directed by Dr. Peter Riola. We have joined our forces together to reach way beyond the USA into Europe, South America and beyond. Bishop Jim Pierce is the overseer of Love Aflame Worldwide which has 150 churches located in the USA, Ghana, Nigeria, Haiti and the Dominican Republic. Love Aflame Worldwide also has three Bible Institutes and one Bible College. Chesapeake Bible College & Seminary is their Bible College. These links which we have outlined began in the later part of the 20th Century and have extended down to 2009. They are only a sample of Chesapeake Bible College & Seminary outreaches.

I received my third doctor's degree, the Doctor of Sacred Letters, on September 30, 2007 from St. Alcuin House Seminary, Blaine, MN. Shirley Comfort also received the Doctor of Philosophy Degree with a major in Nutrition from St. Alcuin's House Seminary. Then in October 24, 2009 I was awarded the Master of Theological Studies in Greek from Chesapeake Bible Seminary. Things were going wonderful for me and I was very fulfilled in my life and ministry. I believed that I was in tremendous health as well as living the overcoming life. Then all of a sudden –yes "suddenly" - I was in for the shock of my life!

Chapter 23

During the night of January 15, 2010 I had a supernatural dream. In this dream the Lord showed me that our ministry was going to be stronger and wider than ever before. I was so amazed with this dream that I wrote it down in my journal. Little did I imagine that only three days later a very dramatic life changing event was going to occur. Then, there it was - suddenly I woke up on Tuesday January 19, 2010 with spasms of the back that were so painful that I screamed every time I moved. The pain was so intense that I could not even get out of the bed. I usually am able to handle pain without too much effort, but this type of pain was something that I had never known before. It was not pain from outside in, but this pain was all internal pain centered in the ribs and spine. So for the next two months I was in and out of this intense pain cycle. Until finally, we had an MRI scan which indicated the diagnosis of **multiple myeloma of the spine.** My wife had spoken to Dr. Brian Clement, director of the Hippocrates Health Institute of West Palm Beach, Florida, about my condition. Dr. Clement told her that we were welcome to come and receive treatments there.

So on March 21, 2010 Shirley and I were accompanied by Derrick Comfort, our oldest son, on a plane headed for West Palm Beach, Florida. After arriving at the Institute, we were met by Alyssa Helene, who promptly gave us our orientation. Our experience at Hippocrates was wonderful. I have never been in such a loving and caring environment. Their program is very intense as it starts early in the morning and continues into the evening. It is a well rounded program of machine therapies, diet, sunshine, counseling, lectures and a series of different kinds of hands on back adjustments. They also have a swimming pool area where they have one pool filled with salt from the Dead Sea in Israel.

God gave me a wide open mission field as I was able to lead to Christ people from Canada, England, Europe and the USA. I shook up every place I went, for Jesus Christ. It was a wonderful opportunity. I witnessed to the Institute Staff, doctors, professors and patients. People come from all over the world to Hippocrates to get well. There are Jews, Hindus, Shintuists, Greek Orthodox, Roman Catholics, Buddhists and every type of free thinker you could imagine that come to Hippocrates. Well, Jesus Christ is the answer to every true seeker of God. God gave us favor with the governing board of the Institute and they gave me a motor scooter to drive back and forth on the campus. As I drove by people, I would say, "Watch out, drunk driver, he is high on Jesus!"

When I would go into a room I would begin singing Christian songs. The people would listen and then come up to me and say, "Could I talk with you in private?" I am interested in the meaning of names, and this provided a wonderful witnessing opportunity. I was able to tell the people what their name meant and then give them a spiritual application. We were there six weeks and actually graduated twice from their three week health institute program. At graduation, Dr. Shirley and I gave our testimony of how Jesus saved us and we sang powerful spiritual songs. People in the audience were wiping tears from their eyes. The Lord gave us five souls for Christ.

My personal trainer was Nancy Fusco Baldwin. Reenie Brewer was also a tremendous help to us. Keith Cini and Jenny Lee were our acupuncture doctors. Kevin, Barry and the ladies of the Therapy Room were such a wonderful help. Rosemary Davila is the Therapy Building Director. She is a sweetheart who Shirley and I love. I only had one serious problem when I was there; **I had so many ladies kiss me on the cheeks that I actually lost count of who they were!** We were at Hippocrates from March 18 through April 24, 2010. When we left, the ladies lined up and left their mark on our cheeks with lipstick kisses. My health had dramatically improved as I went there as a helpless invalid who had lost 40 pounds and 4 inches in health. My weight went from 166 pounds to 126 pounds. My body was in constant pain but when I left, healing had already started in my body.

I wish to thank Derrick Comfort who coordinated most of our flight and arrangements. Derrick actually stayed with us the first week so that we could get acclimated to the new regimen. Janet Reaver came and supported Dr. Shirley for one and a half weeks. Paul Comfort came down and supported his mother in helping me. Paul was with us for five days. Then Sharon Bennett, Shirley's sister, stayed with us for a total of three weeks. Sharon was wonderful and we could never thank her enough for her help. Dr. John Jennings, our adopted chiropractor son, came and visited us. Maria and Marty Bennett, Connie and Bob Caggia, Bill Reaver and Dennis and Rita Wright were among the list of people that came to visit us and supported us with their loving assistance. When we left Hippocrates, we felt that we were leaving family behind.

 Chapter 24

We have known Dennis and Rita Wright for several years and they were also members of the Love Church of Maryland before they moved to Florida. They insisted that we spend time at their Florida home, so we accepted their invitation. It was Saturday, April 24, 2010 and Dennis Wright had come with his van to drive Dr. Shirley and me to his home in North Port, Florida. They have a lovely home with an indoor swimming pool and a very large walking area in which I was able to walk with my walker daily. They also own a health food store where we were able to do some of our shopping.

On Sunday, May 2, 2010 Shirley and I went to church with Dennis and Rita. They are members of the Community Life Church in North Port, Florida. The church is a large multicultural body of believers. The Associate Pastor Kiley Calloway preached that Sunday. After the service he was eager to meet me. The net result of our meeting was that Pastor Calloway is now a student in Chesapeake Bible College & Seminary. He has now already graduated with his Bachelor of Christian Ministry Degree and is scheduled in June 2011 to receive his Master of Theological Studies Degree. He has also requested to be ordained by the College in June 2011.

We met some very wonderful neighbors who live on the same street with the Wrights. We were invited into the home of Dr. Rawl to eat with them. Little did we suspect that their home would be filled with relatives that were eager to meet us. I began witnessing as soon as we got settled in a chair. They were all eager to hear the Word of God, and one of the relatives named Abby had just returned from Iraq. He received Jesus Christ as his Lord and Savior at the supper table as I witnessed to him.

Pastor Ed and Joan Connatser drove down to North Port to bring Shirley back to Maryland. It was on May 17, 2010 that Dennis and Rita Wright drove me to the Sarasota Air Terminal where we boarded a flight to Baltimore Washington International Airport. I had a lot of fun at the Air Port depot witnessing and giving out tracts. Dennis and I sat in the same row of seats and we both enjoyed witnessing to the passenger that sat beside us. Dr. Bob Rundall met us at the B.W.I. terminal and drove me to our home at 14671 Fox Chase Circle, Ridgley, MD. It was three days later that Pastor Ed and Joan brought Shirley home.

So now on January 19, 2011, we have been home ever since that time in Florida. It has been a whole year that I have been fighting the good fight against cancer. I am so grateful for this whole year because I have learned so many wonderful life lessons. This experience has been one of the most rewarding experiences of my whole life. I could have never received the level of blessing and revelation that the Lord has blessed me with, without this warfare. I would have missed so much. I could have gone through life with a strong and healthy body and would have never understood the level of pain that cancer brings to the human body. During this season, I led more people to Christ personally. I have met so many wonderful people and made a host of new friends. I have received more love and care than at any time in my whole life.

The divine purpose in permitting pain is to teach the sufferer the most ultimate and basic truth of the Bible; it is out of human weakness that he experiences divine strength. Apostle Paul could say, "For when I am weak, then am I strong" (II Cor. 12:10). Through my war with this enemy, I have received divine strength. In my agonizing pain, I have been comforted by His grace. He has taken me to where He wanted me all the time! I am, and we all are, in continual need of supernatural power to take us through the trials and traumas of life. "Nay, in all of these things, we are more than conquerors through Him that loved us" (Romans 8:37). Glory!

ABOUT THE AUTHOR

(In pictures)

1. Dr. C at 2 years old
2. Dr. C as a Boy
3. Dr. C – the little soldier
4. Billie, Eleanor, Ronnie
5. Dr. C. and Ronnie
6. Dr. C in sparring pose

ABOUT THE AUTHOR

(In pictures)

7. Dr. C and Boxing Team
8. Dr. C's Parents-in-laws Gordon and Lorraine Evans
9. Dr. C's Dad and Mom Roxy
10. Dr. C's sister Eleanor with Derrick

ABOUT THE AUTHOR

(In pictures)

11. Dr. C at Servicemen's Center
12. Christian Servicemen Center
13. Dr. C sharing gospel at Servicemen's Ctr.
14. Dr. Shirley Evans-Comfort

ABOUT THE AUTHOR

(In pictures)

15. Wedding Day Feb 5, 1960
16. 13 days after birth of 1st son Derrick
17. 4 Generations of Comforts
18. Comfort Family – Derrick and Paul

ABOUT THE AUTHOR

(In pictures)

19. Dr. C's Mom Beatrice
20. Comforts, Children, Grandchildren
21. Comfort Family 1972
22. Dr. C's brother Ron and sister Connie

A Word from *Brother (con't)*

... Dr. Ron Comfort ...

Four children were born to William and Beatrice Comfort. Eleanor was born in 1933 and less than two years later, William Michael entered the family. In 1938, Ronald George was the third in the family; and finally, in 1940, Constance Veronica was the final sibling of the four.

As Billy was four years older than I, I always looked to him as my example. My earliest recollection of our family was when Billy and I were in a gang in Brooklyn. Someone may question how boys of ten and six years of age could be in gangs; however, we lived in an area of Brooklyn where the children were either in a gang or the objects of the gang. Being in a gang, fighting was the norm for each day. There were times when I would pick a fight, and I would get my brother involved to defend me. He was always quick to defend his little brother, Ronnie.

The marriage of William and Beatrice was on the rocks, finally ending in separation and eventually, divorce. While in the military and a patient in the Veterans Hospital in Oteen, NC, Dad had met Roxie Belle King. Because his marriage was not strong, he became enamored with Roxie, and after his divorce, they married. The children in the family were not aware of this until I was seven years old; and Billy, Eleanor, and I were sent to our father in Elmira, New York. Shortly after we were reunited with Dad, he suggested to his new wife that the Comfort family leave New York State and move to Asheville, North Carolina, to begin a new life.

When we got off the bus in Asheville, Dad had one quarter in his pocket. Roxie's Aunt Myrtle Robinson operated a boarding house on Patton Avenue. Since we had no place to live and no money, Aunt Myrtle agreed to allow us to stay at her boarding house until our family could get established. Immediately there was tension between our Dad, a true-born Yankee, and Aunt Myrtle, a thorough-bred southerner. After a brief, but tumultuous time at the boarding house, our family moved to an apartment near William Randolph Elementary School. Eleanor was in the fifth grade, Billy in the fourth grade, and I was in first grade. Many days getting adjusted to the southern culture, I would get in fights with classmates, and Billy, as was always characteristic, would come to my aid. On a more positive note, Billy and I started selling newspapers on the streets of Asheville.

Billy and I had a close relationship even though our home environment was constantly in turmoil. Eleanor, more or less, stayed to herself, being very introverted and quiet. Billy and I got involved in sports and attended baseball games at McCormick Field to watch the Asheville Tourists play. On many occasions we would sneak into the games by climbing over the outfield fences, since we had no money for admission.

I started getting involved in the entertainment field, as Dad somehow was able to manipulate the right people to get me started singing on the radio. Billy did a little of that, but his main interest was in athletics.

It was quite embarrassing to Billy when he got into junior high school and his younger brother followed him to all the junior high events, including the dances and various other forms of entertainment. As a matter of fact, his buddies would say, "Here comes your shadow. Your little brother Ronnie is following you."

In a few years, Billy was captain of a baseball team, and I persuaded him to let me play on the team. Not to hurt his little brother's feelings, he put me in the most unimportant place on the team. I played right field and batted ninth. However, he always tried to include me.

The most pleasant memories that he and I had growing up were during the time we lived on Woodrow Avenue in Asheville. Billy had a newspaper route and rode his new bicycle on his paper route. One day our dad and stepmother got into a serious fight, and Dad decided to leave Roxie and return to Elmira, NY. (By this time, Eleanor had married a young soldier by the name of George Erwin. She married at sixteen years of age, being motivated to get away from our dysfunctional home environment.) I was riding in the car with Dad as we saw Billy returning to the house from his paper route on his bike. Dad said, "Billy, you have a choice. You can either stay with your stepmother or you can go with Ronnie and me to Elmira, NY." Billy left his new bicycle on the street, got into our car, and we headed for Elmira.

Billy, like I, did not like school. Thus, it was not long after moving to Elmira, that Dad encouraged Billy to drop out of school and join the military. Billy was seventeen when he left high school and enlisted in the Air Force. Shortly after Billy had been stationed at Samson Air Force Base in Northern New York, we went to see him upon his completion of basic training. He did not look very good at the time. He had passed out in the chow line and cut his chin requiring stitches. He looked very thin and emaciated. From boot camp, Billy was sent to Panama City, Florida, where his life was totally transformed.

In the meantime, Dad and Roxie reunited and we all moved back to Asheville. In the summer of 1952, I started acting in an outdoor drama, "Thunderland," the life story of Daniel Boone. In that drama, there were many actors and actresses from New York City. I performed in that drama for two summers. As the summer drew to a close, my friends and I decided to drive to Boone, NC, to view a rival play, "Horn in the West." Sunday was our day off, so that was the day that three of my buddies and I traveled to Boone. We had a flat-bed truck in which to travel. Since the seat would hold only three, one was needed to ride on the back of the truck. We rotated positions for awhile, but after I had my turn on the back, I enjoyed it so much that I offered to finish the trip in the back. Having gotten up early in the morning, I became sleepy while riding in the back. I fell asleep and fell off the truck, ricocheting from the truck's tire to the pavement. I lay on the pavement for quite some time, bleeding profusely from a head wound. Finally, a car was flagged down to take me to the hospital in Boone. I was unconscious most of the time, but did wake up briefly to see all the blood on my arms, and then immediately passed out once again. I awakened on the operating table as they were stitching my head, my mouth, and my upper lip. The next morning, when mom and dad came to the hospital to take me home, all my visible body was in bandages except for my right eye. My dad took one look at me and fainted in my stepmother's arms. When I arrived home from the hospital to begin my recuperation, I read in the newspaper about two teenagers who were killed by falling off the back of a truck. That began conviction in my heart and caused me to think about eternity.

Billy had received Christ as Savior when he was stationed in Panama City, FL. One Saturday, as he and his buddy were on the way downtown to get drunk, they stopped and listened to a preacher in an outdoor meeting, and Billy was saved. Immediately, upon his salvation, he went to the barracks and wrote our parents and me a letter telling what had happened to him. When I read the letter, my first impression was that Billy was trying to impress mom and dad. Billy had been somewhat promiscuous in his late junior high and high school days. He had no apprehension about profanity, and it was obvious that he had started to emulate our dad's promiscuous lifestyle. However, in the fall of 1953, Billy came home on furlough, and I noted an amazing change in his life. I was in the ninth grade at David Miller Junior High School when a young soldier entered my home room and asked to see me. It startled me, because I did not immediately recognize him. When Billy went into the military, he had all the trimmings of a worldly teen, and now his appearance was totally different. When he asked to see me, I thought, "Who is he?" All of a sudden, I realized, "This is my brother!"

Billy and I stood on the steps of the school, and he immediately began to witness to me about my need for Christ. I had always paraded my morality, and I thought it was sufficient to take me to heaven. Billy warned me that my pride was going to take me to hell. I was so uncomfortable and under conviction that I encouraged him to go home to see our parents. He was in our home for ten days. Nine out of the ten days, he witnessed to me. Finally, to get him "off my back," I made a profession of faith. However, about two months later during an area-wide meeting in the Asheville City Auditorium, I truly was born again. I was so much under conviction after my brother's fervent witness to me, that I was "ripe for the picking" when the invitation was given.

It was evident that God had called Billy to preach, but he was to be in the military for a four-year stint. He and the people in his church in Panama City began to pray that God would enable him to get an early release from the Air Force that he might enroll in a Christian college to begin his preparation for the ministry. It was a miracle that Billy was discharged two years early, and he immediately enrolled in Bob Jones University.

In the early part of 1954, I hitchhiked to Greenville to visit Billy at college. Billy encouraged me to pray that God would open the door for me to complete my high school years at Bob Jones Academy. I told him that it surely was beyond the realm of possibility, but he encouraged me to pray about it. I think I might have prayed about it one time, because I felt that it would take a miracle equivalent to the Israelite's crossing the Red Sea for me to have the funds for private education.

In the spring of 1953, we moved back to Elmira, NY, and Billy came there for his summer vacation. From the moment he was saved, Billy was consumed with soul winning. When he arrived in Elmira, he immediately began witnessing on the streets. He taught me to win souls by using the Wordless Book. He and I would witness on the street and cause people to think about their eternal destiny. That summer we had the privilege to win many people to Christ.

One day while we were holding a street service, the police stopped us. In the providence of God, Al Shaw, the superintendent of the Elmira Rescue Mission, just across the street from us, saw our plight. After the police stopped us from preaching on the street, Mr. Shaw approached us to see if we would move our preaching into the rescue mission. He said that his basic message was the same as ours, and he invited us to preach in the mission to the homeless and destitute of Elmira. Al Shaw had been saved from a drunkard's life, and God had used him to reach many in his same condition with the Gospel.

Dad had told me that if I went to Bob Jones Academy, he would not send me a penny. In the three years I was in the academy he kept his word and did not send me one cent. At one point during my four years of college, Dad did send me five dollars. However God used the three weeks of meetings in the Elmira Rescue Mission to provide the means for me to enter Bob Jones Academy in the tenth grade. At the conclusion of the last service, Al Shaw called me to the platform and gave me a check for the offerings for the three weeks totaling $150.00. Room, board, and tuition for one year were $750.00, but with the $150.00 I had, God allowed me to enroll.

Billy and I roomed together in that first year. He had a real desire and also sensed a great need to mentor his little brother and to make sure that he did not get side-tracked from his preparation for ministry. I would spend hours in the ping pong room and in extra-curricular activities, and Billy would try to moderate me. Many weekends I went with Billy to Columbia, South Carolina, where he had a fruitful ministry among the military. There were many weekends when Billy would personally win a dozen men to Christ. He continually challenged me to be a soul winner, and to make my first priority being a servant of Christ, preaching the Gospel. Both my salvation and my ministry, since I graduated from college in 1961, have been in a large part due to the influence of my brother.

In my junior year in high school, I stayed during the summer to work on campus. The wages were very meager, and thus I was unable to set aside much for my room, board, and tuition for the fall semester. Billy sold Bibles from house to house that summer in Eastern North Carolina. Since he had the benefit of the GI Bill and did not need very much to supplement the cost of his schooling, he applied his summer's earnings to my school account enabling me to enter my junior year in the academy.

In January, 1957, Billy graduated, and immediately moved to San Antonio, Texas, to work in a Christian Servicemen's Center. Dr. Gilbert Stenholm, the chairman of the Preacher Boys Program, told me that Billy Comfort was the greatest soul winner that Bob Jones University had produced up to that time. I had quite a motivation to try to emulate my brother's soul winning activity. By the time he graduated, he had mentored me to the point where I was able to stand strong, by the grace of God, on my own relationship with Jesus Christ without needing to lean on my brother.

Through the years our relationship has remained strong. God has led us into different avenues of ministry, but we have remained very close. Anyone who has been around Billy has been strongly affected by his soul winning zeal and his love for the Word of God.

In 1989, God led me to start Ambassador Baptist College. The college is simply for the purpose of training young people for full-time Christian service. From the first twenty years of the college ministry, more than seven hundred graduates and former students are involved in ministries around the world. Had it not been for the influence of my brother, Ambassador Baptist College would never have been established. How exciting it will be when we get to heaven and realize all the multitudes that have been influenced through the life, testimony and ministry of Dr. William Comfort.

ABOUT THE AUTHOR

... Dr. William M. Comfort, President ...

Doctor of Philosophy, Oxford Graduate School, Dayton, Tennessee; **Doctor of Sacred Letters**, St. Alcuin House, College of Alcuin of York, Wolsey Hall, Oxford, England; **Doctor of Naturopathy** (with High Honors), Clayton College of Natural Health, Birmingham, Alabama; **Master of Arts**, Capital Bible Seminary, Washington Bible College, Lanham, Maryland; **Master of Letters**, Oxford Graduate School, Dayton, Tennessee; **Master of Theological Studies**, Chesapeake Bible Seminary, Ridgely, Maryland; **Bachelor of Arts**, Bob Jones University, Greenville, South Carolina; **Fellow of the International Biographical Association**, Cambridge, England; **Honorary Fellow of the Anglo American Academy**, Cambridge, England; **Certified Counselor in Personal Behavior Analysis**, Institute for Motivational Living, New Castle, Pennsylvania. **Additional Studies**: Oxford University, Oxford, England; Luther Rice Seminary, Jacksonville, Florida; Hippocrates Health Institute, West Palm Beach, Florida, Teaching Fellow of the Oxford Educational Network, Wolscy Hall, Oxford.

57 years of full time ministry, 50 years of marriage to Dr. Shirley Comfort, two sons and fourteen grandchildren.

CPSIA information can be obtained at www.ICGtesting.com

263664BV00006B/4/P